A SKIN FOR THOUGHT

Interviews with Gilbert Tarrab
on Psychology and Psychoanalysis

Didier Anzieu

A SKIN FOR THOUGHT

Interviews
with Gilbert Tarrab
on Psychology
and Psychoanalysis

Didier Anzieu

translated by
Daphne Nash Briggs

Karnac Books

London   1990   New York

First published in 1990 by
H. Karnac (Books) Ltd.
58 Gloucester Road
London SW7 4QY

Distributed in the United States of America by
Brunner/Mazel, Inc.
19 Union Square West
New York, NY 10003

British Library Cataloguing in Publication Data
Anzieu, Didier
A skin for thought.
 1. Psychoanalysis
 I. Title II. Une peau pour les pensees. *English*
 ISBN 0–946439–86–9

Didier ANZIEU

- Agrégé in philosophy
- Professor Emeritus at the University of Paris-Nanterre
- Honorary President of C.E.F.F.R.A.P.
- Vice-President of the Association Psychanalytique de France
- Director of the collection 'Psychismes' (Paris, Dunod)

Gilbert TARRAB

- Doctor in psychology at the Sorbonne
- Professor in the Department of Administrative Sciences, University of Quebec, Montreal
- Specialist in organizational behaviour and personnel management
- Director of the section 'Organizational Behaviour' at the Department of Administrative Sciences, University of Quebec, Montreal
- Reviewer of scientific books for the papers *La Presse* and *Le Devoir* in Montreal

The authors of this work would like to thank Solange and Claudette Desjardins (of Montreal) and Anne-Marie Clément (of Paris) for their great care and dedication in typing successive versions of the manuscript of these interviews from tape recordings.

CONTENTS

The origins of a psychoanalyst

G T: Didier Anzieu, before we begin in earnest, could you tell us a little about yourself? You were born, I think, at Melun, Seine-et-Marne, on 8 July 1923.

DA: Yes, I came from the Paris area. As a child and adolescent I had the advantage of living in a fairly small town of human proportions, surrounded by fields and forests, while at the same time benefiting from the closeness of Paris. My father's family is Mediterranean. My father—an only child—was born at Sète, a port in Languedoc, where my grandfather was a baker. My mother came from a large family. Her home was a hamlet in Cantal, near Mauriac, in the Massif-Central. My father was accustomed to the sun and the sea; my mother, to a rather harsh continental climate. Their union was a far from . . . temperate one.

GT: Your origins are rather southerly on both sides. . . .

DA: The south of France has remained a constant climatic and cultural point of reference for me. It was an accident of their careers as minor officials (both my father and my mother worked in the administration of Posts and Telecommunications—what was then called the P.T.T.) that brought them together at Melun and led them to marry there. When they did not want me to understand them, they used to speak an Occitan dialect among themselves.

GT: You are an only son, if I am not mistaken.

DA: To be more precise, I am an only child. This undoubtedly goes some way towards explaining why I am attracted to group psychology. One takes an interest in what one has not had. We are driven into action and understanding by what we have lacked.

GT: What you lacked was siblings.

DA: Yes, the group of equals. But there is another side to the picture: an only child is also someone who gets too much, at least that was so for me. It took me time to identify and pinpoint this excess, to lighten the overload, and rid myself of it.

GT: What does an only son have too much of?

DA: His parents' passionate love, their ambitions, anxieties, neuroses, attention, and concern. I should clarify how this 'hypercathexis', as psychoanalysts would say, worked in my case. My arrival into the world was preceded by that of a little sister. . . .

GT: In that case she would surely have been a big sister. . . .

DA: That is true, but I meant that for me she remained definitively little, because she died at birth. You were therefore right to call me 'only son' rather than 'only child'. As things turned out, I never knew her, and I grew up as an only child. But in spirit that was not at all the case. This sister who disappeared, who marked their first setback, remained present for a long time in my parents' thoughts and conversation. I was the second, the one who had to be watched over and tended all the more carefully to shelter him from the miserable fate that had struck the elder. I suffered their fear of repetition. I had to survive at any cost, in order to vindicate my parents. But my survival was problematical in their eyes. The least attack of indigestion or the very slightest draught were threats to me. This put me in a difficult and rather special position. I had to replace a dead sister. So I was not allowed enough life. This was not really a paradoxical situation. Let us call it rather an ambiguous situation.

GT: Were you a cosseted child?

DA: Yes, in the most physical sense of the term. I was not allowed to risk myself in the outside air without being smothered under several layers of clothing: sweater, overcoat, beret, and scarf. The envelopes of care, concern, and warmth with which my parents surrounded me, one upon another, did not part from me even when I left home. I carried their load with me on my back. My vitality was hidden at the heart of an onion, under several outer coverings.

GT: How old were you when you finally rid yourself of these outer layers?

DA: It is too bad if my reply sounds provocative. I was fifty when I became fully aware of it. I then came up with the notion of psychic envelopes, and I published—this was in 1974—my first article on the Skin Ego. This time what became thinkable for me was not what I had lacked but what I had had too much of. In practical life I had not in any case been waiting long enough to 'unmuffle' myself. So far I have given you a one-sided view of my parents. They were not only cautious and anxious. I must give my father his due for having helped me to develop physical and intellectual independence. My father had been a keen sportsman in his youth. He taught me very early on—I think I was three and one-half—to keep my balance on a little bicycle. I still remember that I could push off and roll along but not stop at all. He would sprint in front of me, get off his bike, and catch me as I passed by. Later on, on the weekly day off school, which then fell on a Thursday, he made arrangements to be free in the afternoon, and we would go together for long bicycle rides along the banks of the Seine or in the forest of Fontainebleau. Later still I went out alone or with my school friends. My father put me down for the local tennis club, while 'forgetting' to get me lessons; I have persisted with this sport to this very day, with the same awkwardnesses and the same beginner's illusions. . . . But I am getting away from your question. How did I react to the muffling? I became increasingly intolerant of anything stifling, and I responded fairly swiftly with temper outbursts.

GT: With temper outbursts?

DA: Yes. I had a reputation for a bad temper. Temper outbursts were my principal defect as far as my parents were concerned. For a long time I have no idea where these brutal explosions came from. They persisted until my second analysis. I then understood that they were my way of loosening the constraint, of taking air and space, and of making myself some room. Besides, although these outbursts were violent, they did not leave behind too bitter a taste in my mouth. I felt moderately guilty about them. But they often—too often— made people around me suffer, as a child and then as an adult. This suffering I have inflicted is one of the principal regrets of my existence. What is more, my father set me the example of violent fits of temper, sometimes against my mother and sometimes against myself.

GT: Your father was very important to you at that time, more so than your mother. . . .

DA: Both my parents were equally important, but in different ways. My father René was a practical, active, materialist man. My mother Marguerite had intellectual tastes and gifts that I certainly inherited. On the other hand, everyday reality only concerned her superficially. Her discord with my father entrenched itself in this area, with her negligent, whimsical, out-of-proportion attitude towards material tasks. Sometimes she would do a lot, and at other times she would immerse herself in a book and forget the rest. Still on the subject of my mother, it is she who is responsible for my being drawn towards psychology and psychoanalysis. Some time after my birth she suffered a nervous 'breakdown'. . . .

GT: A depression. . . .

DA: Yes, a nervous depression; and if I used an English term with you, something I never do and which is out of place when speaking to a French Canadian like yourself, it is the sign that a strong emotion has been awakened in me. Let me be precise, at whatever cost: a depression accompanied by persecutory manifestations that made life more and more impossible around her. She had to be hospitalized twice, on the second occasion for rather a long time. So I was separated from her first of all at eighteen months, then at around the age of four to five. I was brought up by one of my mother's sisters, who happened to be my godmother. Her husband had died as a result of his injuries shortly after the First World War. She could not have children, and my parents took her in. She attached herself to me and also to my father, and her

increasingly important role in the household added to the
tension that prevailed between my father and mother
because of their imcompatible characters. This was a sort of
vicious circle. Dispossessed progressively of her husband and
her son, my mother lost the means of defending herself
against her own latent pathology, and when it broke through
openly, this precipitated my father's decision to separate
from my mother and thereafter to live with his sister-in-law,
not without keen feelings of guilt. My Oedipus complex was
sharpened by this, and became even more 'complex'.

GT: So you have few memories of your mother?

DA: Yes and no. My father and godmother talked about her
to me. I resumed regular contact with her after my marriage.
On several occasions she mentioned her childhood and mine.
But it has been more through slow self-analytical work than
through my two psychoanalyses that I have been able to
reconstruct in my mind the difficulties that my mother had
in contact with me during the first months of my life. I would
lurch—as I said a little while ago—from too much to too
little, from too little to too much. Sometimes she would force
excessive care upon me, to the point of causing pain, and
over-rich food that she had to 'give' me: with these physical
excesses she was undoubtedly making up for her inability to
show affection and to demonstrate tenderness. At other
times she would cut off, turn in on herself, forget my presence
and my needs, and let feeding time pass by. Apparently I
cleaned the wheel of my pram with a finger and then scru-
pulously sucked the grease without her noticing: it is this
incident that decided my godmother to take charge of me.
Madness very quickly became a domestic reality for me, full
of problems, heavy with menace, but a reality that I could
and still can face up to with resolution. Freud explains the
attraction of imaginative literature in terms of 'disquieting
strangeness'. For me, madness was an experience of 'disquieting familiarity'. As an adolescent I was afraid I might

be victim of a possible hereditary trait. After my first analysis this fear faded, and I wanted to understand what happened to my mother.

GT: What became of your mother after she finally left
hospital?

DA: In the end she led an independent life after years of
confinement. She worked hard to supplement the two mea-
ger pensions that my father and the P.T.T. paid her. She then
devoted herself to charitable works, in which she was much
liked and sometimes rather touchy. Right up to the end of her
life she retained an insatiable intellectual curiosity. At
eighty years of age she embarked on writing a long poem in
classical form on the women in the Bible. After my marriage,
as I said, I wanted to find her again in all the senses of the
word: to renew contact with her, and to feel like a son with his
mother. Our meetings became increasingly satisfying for her
and for me—except when her persecutory mistrust returned.
My father died in 1967. My mother lived until 1981. I learned
to understand her, calm her, and help her re-establish per-
manently an unstable equilibrium. I served her as a reliable
link with a reality that would otherwise have remained
frightening and unsteady for her.

GT: You were saying that your relationship with your
father was very different. . . .

DA: If I was able to hold out, despite being marked by the
presence of a mother who had her moments of madness, and
to resist the contagion and avoid mental illness—I believe I
got away with an ordinary neurosis—it was because of my
solid and warm relationship with my father. He overflowed
with affection. He sustained me throughout all my childhood, and afterwards in many of my adult undertakings. My
father lost his own father at the age of twelve, and until I was
twelve myself we were close to one another. He passed on to

me the best of his prematurely interrupted relationship with his own father. With puberty, my crisis of opposition to my family setting, characteristic of that age, was accentuated by the need, which had by then become imperative, to shake off the stifling surveillance and infantilizing care that I was subjected to. There were years of tension between him and me. But in order to achieve my masculine identity, it was a good thing that he put up resistance to me. He had suffered in life. His mother died a few years after his father. Orphaned completely at seventeen years of age, he hastily took the entrance examination for the postal service, and he climbed the successive rungs of its administrative ladder, up to that of inspector. His wish, which I fulfilled, was that I should take as far as possible the studies that he himself regretted having abandoned. Geography was the most important subject for becoming a postman, knowledge of all the countries of the world and their big towns, and knowledge of sea routes and railways for the dispatch of the mail. Together with the clarinet and the bicycle it remained one of his favourite activities. During the walks that he and I took together at a steady pace among the fields and woods around Melun, my father would parade these foreign countries in conversation, down to the very smallest and most distant, and he would question me on the names of their capitals. This game stimulated my appetite for knowledge. I travelled the whole world while walking and chatting with him. This perhaps accounts for my small appetite for actual travels. . . .

GT: M Anzieu, I would like, if that's all right, to return to what you yourself call this episode of madness in your mother. It is undoubtedly a painful experience to call to mind. Could we perhaps stop a moment at the reasons for her depression? It had never happened before, I presume?

DA: Not to my knowledge. . . .

GT: What happened at that point?

DA: You are asking me a delicate question. I can hardly give you an account of what I experienced at a time when I was not sufficiently aware and was incapable of distinguishing between what was going on inside myself and what was going on around me. I talked about it as an adolescent with the family doctor; then with my mother at the end of her life. I have thought a lot about it, and I believe what happened was as follows: My mother came from a family of seven children. She was seen as the difficult child. Her father, therefore my grandfather, when she told him about her plans to marry the man who was going to be my father, seems to have tried to dissuade her: 'You are not made for marriage.' And he even seems to have warned my father, who later often regretted having remained deaf to the warning. My mother was beautiful and educated. She did not look like a peasant girl, although that was her original background. She was self-taught, she devoured books, she learned foreign languages—at the end of her life she started to study Breton—and she had a lovely style of writing. She was very pleasing to my father, and they fell in love.

But I am getting away from your question. Why her depression? Because of her fragile character. This fragility prevented her from facing up to my birth, which re-activated in her the catastrophic memory of the stillborn baby. Why this fragile character? I think it was due to the circumstance of her own birth. She was the third child of her sibling group, the third or the fourth . . . therein lies the problem. Three girls were in fact born before her. The family lived in a big stone house, near the stable and the fields. The living room was the only one with heating, in a large fireplace where big pieces of wood were burnt, where food was cooked, and inside which one could sit on benches. What follows happened before my mother was born. It was a feast day. Marguerite, the youngest of the three girls, had been dressed in an organdy frock to go to Mass. She had been left for a moment in the charge of the eldest, the one who was to be my god-mother. The little one was lightly clad, it was cold, and she went close to the fire . . . and she died, burnt alive. This was an appalling shock for her parents and for her two sisters. My mother was then conceived to replace the dead child. And since yet another girl was born, she was given the same name, Marguerite—the living dead, in a way. . . . It is no accident that my mother spent her life multiplying means of escaping the flames of Hell. . . . This could be called submitting to her fate, a tragic fate. Only on one occasion did my mother talk openly about it to me. But I knew about it through family legend. I think her depression stemmed from this unstable role. She set it aside after the birth of her dead little girl, a relentless repetition of her fate. And my successful birth reactivated the unbearable threat. . . .

GT: You mentioned at the beginning of the interview that you owe your present profession as a psychologist and psychoanalyst above all to your mother.

DA: I could hazard a banal formulation, but one that seems true so far as I personally am concerned. I became a psychoanalyst in order to take care of my mother. Not so much in order to take care of her in reality, although I did succeed in the last quarter of her life in helping her to find a relatively happy and balanced existence. I mean: taking care of my mother in myself and in others. Taking care of them of this threatening and threatened mother. . . .

GT: You were involved with her right up to the last moment. . . .

DA: My wife and I were with her until two hours before her death.

GT: Did she live with you?

DA: Neither she nor we could have tolerated that. For the sake of her own balance she needed to live alone, in her own house.

GT: We shall have the opportunity to return to the issue of the walls of the asylum, but since we are on the subject of your relationship with your mother and her being locked up—you yourself used the expression—for psychiatric reasons: how did your mother experience being locked up at that period?

DA: That was around the 1930s. Legislation, prevailing ideas, methods of care, and lifestyles were different to those of today. Officially, as a child raised by my father and godmother, I only knew that my mother was away, that she was not well, that she needed to get better, and that there were threats in the air. I was alerted to the danger of 'kidnapping'—again an English word, you see, when we broach a subject that disturbs me. . . . As for her hospitalization, there is what my mother said and what actually happened. What happened was I think beneficial for her in the medium term. She lived in a protected environment. The doctors and nurses were attentive to her case. This was enough to stabilize her state of mind and prevent her persecutory tendencies from organizing themselves into a lasting delusion. At that time there were no drugs that acted on disturbances of mood, and psychotherapy was a shambles. Perhaps one day I shall relate what she told me about the later phase of her medical contact with the young psychiatrists of the day at Sainte-Anne, notably Jacques Lacan and Daniel Lagache, and her later working relationships at Jacques Lacan's father's house. My mother was intelligent and full of curiosity. At the hospital she was given the task of running the library. She could read to her heart's content. She resumed her studies, which she had taken as far as the certificate of secondary education. She presented herself for the baccalauréat, which she only just failed. These are the facts. By contrast, what she said has a different tone. It was the humiliation of being interned, being prevented from living her life, the horror of constant mixing with her dormitory mates, whom she called the 'real' patients, because she herself never considered herself as one. She had a sense of her own fragility, and of mistakes that she might have made, but she considered that she had been placed there wrongly. Her life was a sort of Hell. Nonetheless, she established firm bonds with her companions in misery, which endured after each of them had resumed an autonomous life.

GT: Could I lead off from this example to ask you for your thoughts about what is generally called the walls of the asylum? Is locking people up a viable solution in the more or less long term? Have you considered this question as a psychoanalyst? What do you think about what Laing and Cooper, to cite only the best-known names in anti-psychiatry, denounce in their books?

DA: Whether it is the effect of the onslaught of anti-psychiatry or the result of the development of individual and collective psychotherapies as well as psychopharmacology, long-term internment has become an exceptional measure. In any case, we use different terms: hospitalization, placement, etc.

GT: With hindsight, would you say that it would have been in your mother's interest not to have gone through this confinement?

DA: That is an insoluble question. The battery of knowledge, techniques, and means of action is so different now, as also are the attitudes of the public and the medical profession towards mental illness. In 1930 psychoanalysis had only just begun to be practised in France, and more specifically in Paris. The first psychoanalysts to work at Melun had scarcely appeared before 1970. At that time there were none of the props that now exist and which would undoubtedly have given my mother more help in protecting her psychic equilibrium.

GT: So her confinement was inevitable. . . .

DA: I find it difficult to reply. What one does nowadays, and what I find myself doing successfully with patients in my care who are going through very difficult moments, intense crises of anxiety, or are on the brink of a delusional episode, is to alternate psychotherapy with drug treatment given by a doctor who takes responsibility for it in agreement with me, and even to organize a short stay in hospital.

An uncertain psychologist

G T: Now we will move on to your adolescence and your first intellectual interests. They were not, I think, directly connected with psychoanalysis or psychology. At the beginning you turned towards philosophy. . . .

DA: I have always read a lot, and at that point in my life I read a large number of philosophical works. I shared this taste for reading with my mother, but it was encouraged by my father: reading was a way of reuniting my parents, who were out of tune with one another.

We lived not in poverty, but somewhat frugally. All the same, so far as books that I asked to buy were concerned, my father was never stingy. What is more, I forged an excellent relationship with a bookseller in Melun, young and open, who did not confine himself to buying textbooks and popular fiction. I spent several hours every week in his shop. He let me browse on his shelves, leaf at length through a volume that interested me, and even take it home, as he knew that my father would settle the account.

The big intellectual discovery that I made in adolescence was in philosophy class at the Collège Jacques Amyot at Melun. The teacher, Alexandre Champeau, was a disciple of Auguste Comte. As a positivist, he was interested in all branches of knowledge. He knew how to get close to his pupils. He led us to read and to write. I became familiar with thinkers as widely separated as Descartes and Hume. I swung between rationalism and empiricism, until the latter system ended up getting my vote. Champeau gave us a very full course in psychology, although Freud was only mentioned in passing. Up to that point I had wavered between Letters and Sciences. I was what is called a 'good student', equally able in both domains. What is more, I have retained interest in and admiration for scientific discoveries, and I remain fascinated by the progress of human knowledge about matter and life. I am not happy with the unfortunate split that has become entrenched in France between Letters and Sciences. At that time, the baccalauréat was taken over two years. After having passed the first part with distinction, I had to decide between elementary mathematics and philosophy–letters. I opted for the latter, doubtless because I sensed the enlightenment I would find in it, which corresponded with my subconscious expectations.

There, I discovered the world of thought. The class was mixed, and I met the girl who was to be my wife. Champeau put me in for the Concours Général des Lycées et Collèges, and I obtained a *proxime accessit* in the philosophical dissertation. At this little provincial college this was a glorious moment. I certainly enjoyed the event, but I glimpsed what could be the vanity of seeking glory for its own sake, and since then I have remained suspicious of both of them— vanity and glory alike.

GT: Your way ahead was all marked out. . . .

DA: Yes, I was on the rails: the upper first class (hypo-khagne and khagne) at the Lycée Henri IV at Paris, the École Normale Supérieure in the rue d'Ulm, and agrégation in philosphy. All the same, it was a journey marked by setbacks. I had to take each of these two examinations twice before passing them, and I was the second last to be admitted to the E.N.S.-Lettres in the 1944 examination (postponed until 1945 because of the war). I was drawn towards teaching from a very early age. When I was 10, in my last year at primary school, the teacher gave as an essay subject the job we would like to do. Instead of writing 'professeur agrégé' I wrote professeur 'abrégé'. Doubtless the castration complex was at work in me. . . .

GT: Your way ahead was marked out by your father. . . .

DA: My father in the flesh and my successive fathers in the spirit: a primary teacher called Dionne, secondary teachers like Champeau, and yet another—it is now time for me to talk to you about him. My father had the original, excellent idea of getting me special tuition not in the subjects in which I was weak, but in the one I turned out to be strongest in, in order to help me to do as well as possible. Starting out from a small provincial college, I had to be equipped to face the rough competition of a large Parisian lycée. My father there-fore approached a professor of French who had retired from the Collège de Melun and who had devoted himself for some years to deciphering and editing the manuscript of Pascal's *Pensées* for publication. Zacharie Tourneur had had his the-sis project turned down at the Sorbonne because he was attacking the Brunschvicg edition, which was then author-itative. He had rediscovered the plan that Pascal had con-ceived, and instead of giving himself up to the intellectual game that consisted in each editor classifying the fragments according to an arbitrary personal order, he published the *Pensées* with Vrin and in the Éditions de Cluny according to the classification that the author had himself embarked upon, and which was interrupted by his premature death.

GT: You were his spiritual son. . . .

DA: I felt myself to be son of Pascal and of Tourneur. The latter initiated me into how to read a manuscript, into the need for palaeographical and philogical rigour, into research in historical sources, into the epistemological break that detached Pascal from the influence of the intellectual milieu of his father's friends, into the deconstruction that he applied to their world system, and into his discovery of a history of man that took account of the grandeur and misery of our condition. He involved me in the work of revision of his edition of the *Pensées* when the first had gone out of print. For several years I dreamed of writing the thesis that he had failed to see through, on Pascal's philosphical system, until I realized that this dream was fulfilling his wish rather than mine. By contrast, he cultivated in me several qualitites that were to last: clarity of thought and sobriety in writing. Tourneur, after our first interview, gave me a dissertation subject whose title I have forgotten. I was in such a state of exaltation at being accepted and put to the test by a master like himself that I let myself be carried away by my writing. I produced a long, wordy text, overladen with rather heavy stylistic effects, of which I was not a little proud.

GT: How old were you then?

DA: I was seventeen. Tourneur was dry and serious: 'My little Didier, let's get something straight between us; if you want to go in for journalism, you need to approach someone else.' This was a terrible humiliation, but fruitful. I set to work more seriously and coolly. Since then I have on a number of occasions verified that euphoria and enthusiasm can be deceptive states.

GT: M Anzieu, how did psychoanalysis emerge in all this?
When did you move away from philosophy?

DA: Philosophy led me to psychoanalysis. I was in khagne
at the Lycée Henri IV. There, too, I found teachers who had a
high opinion of me and encouraged me.

GT: They were guiding lights on your way.

DA: Jean Hyppolite opened Hegel to us. Ferdinand Alquié
touched on the surrealists. He had had a psychoanalysis and
spoke of it in a way that was partly critical and partly
sympathetic. On his advice I read the *Introductory Lectures
on Psycho-Analysis*. In them, Freud described something
that I felt and which no-one, neither my parents nor my
teachers apart from Alquié, had echoed back to me. In short, I
found myself there. It was a new geography that took the
place of the one that my father had taught me. I had a map
with which to orientate myself within the internal continent.
Regions were defined to which names were given, with frontiers and lines of communication. Movements of body and
soul that I had up to that point simply suffered, could now be
identified, localized, and mastered.

GT: M Anzieu, you have written that you pursue your
current profession, psychoanalysis, for want of any other.
You have always wanted to write. You would have preferred
to be a writer.

DA: In order to dedicate oneself to the profession of writing
it is necessary to be a dedicated writer. Literary practice is no
more to me than Ingres' violin. In class, every fortnight
Champeau gave us a philosophy dissertation to prepare with
two subjects to choose from; I often covered both, even if I
only turned in one script. I have always written a lot: a
personal diary, letters, poems, fiction—but in the form of

fragments and drafts. I have started my autobiography ten times. I have never finished what could be a long-winded work. I have lacked talent and time. But this has given me a facility in writing and helps me to attend to my style when I write a book or a psychoanalytic article. Once I attempted a collage–montage of what I regarded as my best literary texts. This did not come to anything. Another time I embarked upon rewriting the *Aeneid* on the model of the group dynamics of the 1960s. The twelve books were to be matched by accounts of twelve meetings of a group of nine persons (hence an 'ennead'—you see the play on words), gathered together without knowing one another in advance, and with no other rule than to talk together about what they felt in that situation. The series of shared emotions that they were supposed to experience would repeat those of Aeneas and his companions. In my prose account I interpolated long passages translated from Virgil: I did not know that this was called intertextuality.

When I read extracts of this to my wife, I had never seen her pull such a long face. It was an indigestible mass. With *The Name of the Rose*, in which he describes seven symbolic days of collective psychology in a 'seminary' (in the religious sense), Umberto Eco has published the book that I would have loved to have spent ten years of my life in conceiving.

GT: You do write stories, all the same. . . .

DA: I have in fact published the *Contes à rebours* [Contrary Stories] (Christian Bourgois, 1975). It is the only literary form in which I have succeeded in composing texts presentable to the public, doubtless because of their brevity. I embarked upon my first fictional story at twelve years of age. It was a pornographic novel. The title, *Les Guerres bitiques*, was a parody of the Punic wars that we were studying with the Latin teacher. *La bite*, to describe the male organ, was the most obscene term that I and my friends knew. I made the virile penis into the warrior weapon *par excellence*. It was an obvious elaboration of an infantile sexual theory. I secured undoubted prestige among my classmates at the Collège Jacques Amyot by circulating the pages of this novel, which I soon made haste to destroy in order to ward off the ultimately dangerous consequences of my own success. If grown-ups had got their hands upon it . . .! Hadn't my father and godmother found in one of my pockets (that they were in the habit of inspecting) a drawing that reading from this novel had inspired in the boy who sat next to me, and which, without any shadow of doubt, represented a penis . . . in an illustrated strip! On that occasion I was given a slap, the most resounding that I remember. With my parents there was a 'blackout'—again an English word—where sexual issues were concerned. My first literary venture—and several others that followed it—responded to that by a provocative defiance, while at the same time expressing my vital need to imagine.

During my growing years, I had a wish that was even more important than that of being a writer, and that was the wish to be an actor. One can always play other people's texts if one cannot write them oneself. On Sunday afternoons, in his room that served as drawing room and was drenched in sunlight, my father used to read aloud to my godmother and me: and all the theatre of Edmond Rostand passed before us. From this I derived that temptation to gradiloquence that Tourneur knew how to combat. At the Lycée Henri IV and the École Normale Supérieure I took an active part in the end-of-year reviews. I played opposite Pontalis in *Ubi-Roi*. During my military service, at the regimental entertainment, I put on Camus's *Caligula*, whose text had just appeared as a book but which had not yet been staged.

GT: Did you act the part of Caligula?

DA: Of course. My taste for psychodrama is the logical extension of all this. For the sake of my personal equilibrium I need something else than to stay seated for hours on end in

my analyst's chair. For a long time psychodrama has in part
responded to this need.

GT: You who are known as a very orthodox analyst—how
does one explain these contrasting sides of your personality:
actor, artist, and aesthete? You are interested in aesthetics,
you have published stories, you have embarked upon novels,
you have a strong taste for play; on the other hand, you give
the impression of being a psychoanalyst who is closed in and
even somewhat rigid. We are in the presence of two different
characters.

DA: I am not really in a position to offer you an explanation. It would rather be up to you to do that. I can simply state
that I do function like that. One of my problems is to organize
my life in a way that is sufficiently varied, providing niches
for both aspects to find satisfaction.

GT: Let us pursue the course of your career. You therefore
started to take an interest in psychoanalytic texts and then
went on to train in that profession?

DA: The class of 1944—which I was in at the École Normale Supérieure—had a certain number of enthusiasms; for
some it was mathematical logic (Jean-Toussaint Desanti
was among our lecturers), for others it was Marxism
(Althusser was the most significant example, and also the
most dramatic); and finally for Laplanche, myself, and several of my friends, it was psychology, psychiatry, and psychoanalysis. Maurice Merleau-Ponty, whose *Phenomenology of
Perception* had recently made him famous, taught us a
course. Another lecturer, Georges Gusdorf, invited people
like Daumezon and Lacan to give papers, which introduced
us to various aspects of psychopathology.

GT: Lacan, already. . . .

DA: Between 1945 and 1947 it was Lacan before Lacanism.
By the same token, a very lively and healthy antagonism
between Freudians and Marxists came before the Freudian–
Marxist soup that was served up to us later. On the whole I
was disappointed by the three years I spent at the rue d'Ulm.
At least, by the intellectual vacuum that I found in the place
of all that my discovery of philosophy had led me to expect. I
was hoping for thinkers: what I found was historians, com-
mentators, and scholiasts. Worse still, the exercises that we
were made to do trained us to talk about anything, no matter
what. Philosophy was degraded into an inferior form of rhetoric. This was my second disappointment in love, after that
for my mother. In that setting, one prided oneself above all
upon being original. Scarcely anyone was concerned about
being truthful. My 'scientific' spirit was not satisfied with
this. In my eyes, philosophy represented the search for a
certain truth about man, which presupposes method and
proof. I probably also lacked a fundamentally philosophical
temperament. However that may be, I demanded from psychology and then psychoanalysis what philosophy failed to
deliver me. My career choice became definite. While I was
working for my diploma in higher studies in philosophy on
Pascal's political thought, I followed the courses that Paul
Guillaume gave at the Sorbonne-Lettres on animal psychology and Gestalt theory, and classes on psycho-physiology at
Sorbonne-Sciences. After my success in the agrégation in
philosophy in 1948, I decided not to take up a post immediately, and with my wife's agreement (we had just married) I
decided to remain for a year in Paris and to get private
tuition to prepare with her for teaching certificates in psychology, which had then just been instituted, as well as for
the diploma of the Institut de Psychologie, which gave us a
more concrete training. We followed presentations of
patients at the Hôpital Sainte-Anne, and we learned to use
projective tests. I entered the Centre psycho-pédagogique
Claude Bernard, the first of its kind in France, which

Juliette Favez-Boutonier and Georges Mauco had just founded. I tested children, I did initial interviews with parents, I was present at examinations by the doctor–psychiatrist and case discussions, I discovered psychodrama with Mireille Monod and Evelyne Kestemberg, then Philippe Gravel and Geneviève Testemale. Meanwhile, André Berge became medical director of the centre. I was a trainee psychologist in Pr. de Graciansky's dermatological unit, where I administered Rorschach tests to excema patients at the Hôpital Saint-Louis: there I had my first, though still vague, inkling of the skin ego.

GT: This was between the years 1946 and 1950. What were you doing during the war, from 1939 to 1945?

DA: I was working for the baccalauréat and I started higher studies. I lived at Melun, in an occupied zone, then I boarded at the Lycée Henri IV in Paris. I did the written section of the first part of the baccalauréat twice—first at the end of May 1940 in Paris, when the German offensive began (I was not yet seventeen years of age), and the oral could not take place, nor the results be published. And I began again in September at Montpellier after the exodus that took me to a paternal great-aunt at Sète, the native town of Valéry, with whom my father had been a fellow pupil at the Lycée; it was also the town of Jean Vilar and George Brassens. Melun had other associations for me: Jacques Amyot, Renaissance Hellenist and humanist, was born there; and Abelard, theologian and philosopher of the Middle Ages, taught there. And his wretched sexual fate tempted me to compensate for my own castration complex, which I had just begun to be aware of in the course of my incipient practice of psychodrama and my first psychoanalysis, by slogging away at my studies. These two thinkers had names beginning with the letter A: and my fallacious pride would from time to time whisper that there are never two without three.

GT: From seventeen to twenty-one years of age you lived under the German jack-boot. What memories do you have of that? Did you sympathize with the Resistance? Were you politicized?

DA: Until 1942 almost all the world around me was crushed by defeat. It was a matter of survival, material and intellectual, avoiding heedless risks, being on one's guard against the Germans, and, in expectation of the return of better days, of preserving by means of dogged hard work all that could be preserved and that might be useful in the future. I learned about the appeal of the 18th of June several days after De Gaulle had made it. We listened to English radio in the family or among friends. There were few distractions, and it was impossible to go out in the evening because of the curfew. There was internal and external austerity, and, on the political plane, passivity reigned in my family and educational circle. After the Japanese attack on Pearl Harbour which made the entry of the United States into the war inevitable, the climate was transformed: immense hopes became possible once more. We could lift our heads again, because the Americans would land one day and liberate us. My father was in both wars, in 1914–18 and 1939–40. He had bad memories of both, which he did not like to recall. He tended to encourage me to be careful. I had sympathies for the Resistance, but I was not actively involved in it.

GT: Let us return to 1950. You were in practice as a psychologist, and you trained in psychodrama on which you were to write your first book in 1957. And then?

DA: Daniel Lagache replaced Paul Guillaume in the chair of psychology at the Sorbonne and instituted the *licence de psychologie* in France. He encouraged me to take it. I had met him by taking his course, which was intended for candidates for the agrégation in philosophy. I wrote a paper that pleased him, in which I compared the Jacksonian model of the nervous system with the Freudian model of the psychic apparatus. He took me into his friendship and helped me administratively to remain in Paris after the agrégation, to pursue my specialization in psychology. He gave me a subject for a major thesis with a view to the Doctorat d'État: 'Self-analysis', which took the place of my initial project on 'Pascal's thought'. At that time the Doctorat ès Lettres involved two theses. For the subject of my minor thesis I proposed psychodrama. Since my work was going well, Lagache took me on as assistant in 1951. I asked him whether it was necessary, in order to practise clinical psychology, for me to do medical studies, like Wallon, Juliette Boutonier, himself, and many others had done. He said it was not. When I had informed him of my interest in psychoanalysis and my wish eventually to become a psychoanalyst, he was explicit: 'There is only one way ahead to consider: and that is to have an analysis yourself.' He naturally refused when I approached him as an analyst. And I made a preliminary round of the members of the Training Commission of the Société Psychanalytique de Paris to be taken on to begin a training analysis. In his integrity and rigour, this man refused to give any advice about the choice of my future analyst. I had heard Lacan at the École Normale Supérieure. He had come to give a curious talk on identification. He had brought two glass tubes, in each of which he had a migratory locust—one that lived as an isolated individual, and another that belonged to a swarm. He showed us the morphological changes that gregarious life brought about in the animal, driving it to resemble its fellow locusts. He already had a quasi-instinctive sense of group effects and their production. . . . When I met Lacan in his study, while I was going the rounds that I have just mentioned, and when I had told him that I was at the École Normale Supérieure, an agrégé and a philosopher, he offered to take me immediately into psychoanalysis. I was rather thrown, and rather dazed by a well-known man attaching importance to my little person. My paternal complex was set going again. I let myself embark upon it. . . .

GT: In Lacan you found an *N*th father.

DA: I started with him in the first days of January 1949, at three sessions a week and at a very reasonable fee, adapted to my modest income—an analysis that was to last four years.

GT: You therefore know Lacan from the inside?

DA: It is true that a patient ends up by acquiring an intuitive knowledge of his analyst's mental functioning. This cannot be reduced to projections or to the transference that he has to him. The acquisition of such knowledge is even one of the criteria for terminating an analysis. A psychoanalyst is not superhuman, except when the regressive urge provoked by treatment reactivates the infantile idealization that the patient had once held for his parents. He is a man like other men, who would not have come to analysis if he had not suffered from certain internal conflicts, and if he had not retained certain marks from the dramas of his history, while at the same time having achieved a relative detachment from these conflicts and dramas. He is someone who needs, in order to go on living, to work in close contact with the unconscious, his own through that of others.

In short, at the same time as I was making a positive and intense paternal transference to Lacan, which allowed me to talk to him volubly and comfortingly about things that I had never said to anyone, I was surprised by this or that in his behaviour. At the beginning of my treatment he gave me sessions of a normal length—of forty to forty-five minutes— and he saw me at the agreed times. After two years of work with him, the analytic setting suffered some knocks. The length of sessions was reduced to thirty and then to twenty minutes. The waiting room filled with people anxious to know whether they would be seen—Lacan would open the door and point to the chosen one, who would cross the room again ten or fifteen minutes later to leave. I would read. Lacan would tap my shoulder, and it was my turn to pass in front of everyone or to find myself postponed to another day. . . . The Master, wrenching a great sigh from himself, would take me into his confidence like a friend, saying that he was snowed under, that he had to get to an unforeseen meeting or deal with a difficult case, implying that I wasn't one, and that I could therefore come back at another time, and that he was sure I understood. This reinforced my narcissism, which anyway had no need of it, and made it difficult for me to express my astonishment, criticism, and disagreement, or in other words a negative transference, without the elaboration of which a psychoanalysis is not complete.

During sessions, Lacan was intermittently attentive. Sometimes, instead of sitting in his analytical chair, he would pace the room in order to stretch his legs, or pick up a book; he would sit at his desk, where he would read—for instance, leafing through pages covered with Chinese characters, since it seemed he was learning the language (if the unconscious is structured like a language, and a written language, what singularities does the unconscious of the Chinese derive from their pictograms?). Sometimes his maid would come and knock on the door to bring tea or sandwiches, to take away the mail, or to let him know that he had a telephone call. Lacan would give instructions for her to reply, or would even go to answer himself. 'But don't let that stop you from continuing your session in my absence', he once tossed out at me as he disappeared from his consulting room.

I very much like surrealist games. I vaguely knew that Lacan mixed with the surrealists. But for me, psychoanalysis was a serious affair. There was no way that it could be assimilated to the spoofs that abounded among students of the École Normale Supérieure and in which I had taken my part. Play is play. Work, which involves associating, linking, becoming aware, and interpreting, demands seriousness, and attention and respect for the other person.

My confidence in Lacan deteriorated after two trying episodes. He invited me to follow his seminar when I was not asking him for anything; I was simply talking to him about a friend who attended it. I was going to say that there were perhaps counter-indications for a person being taught by someone with whom he was in psychoanalysis, but he forestalled my objection: at the point I had reached, there was no problem, and I could come. Once again I had the impression that he was making an exception for me because of merits that were not apparent to me with the certainty they appeared to have for him. Once again I was to find, when exchanging confidences with friends after our respective analyses with him were ended, that he had made the same offers to them, and that there were dozens of us that he had tried to attach to him by letting us believe that each of us was an exceptional case in his eyes.

So I went to this seminar. At the end, the discussion continued among the audience. A woman colleague at the Centre Psycho-pédagogique made critical remarks about what we had just heard on the subject of the transference. At my next session, I told Lacan that there had been criticisms. 'Who?', he asked. I was thrown. In response to my silence, he insisted upon the rule of omitting nothing: it is important to use people's names in psychoanalysis; in any case, I think I know who it is. Was psychoanalysis to become one of the modern forms of delation? I no longer remember whether I 'gave' the name of the culprit. What I do know is that from then on I kept my criticisms to myself, I repressed my negative transference that this man obviously could not tolerate, and I was impatient for one thing only—that this psychoanalysis, which was getting bogged down, should come to an end. Most of my analytical siblings subsequently shared similar confidences with me.

GT: It was really no longer any good. . . .

DA: One last disillusionment. When I asked that we finish, Lacan not only offered no interpretation (in four years I had heard two or three interpretations from him all told, and even then in allusive form), but he acquiesced straight away: my sessions were reduced in number from three to two and then to one. But he made me 'pay' for this concession: 'To ensure that you will go on making the same effort, you will continue to pay me the same amount each week as you did when you had three sessions.' At the same time he invited me to get my training analysis validated by returning to see the members of the Training Commission of the S.P.P. A fortnight later I told him that I had a first meeting. He stopped me on the doorstep, put his hand on my shoulder in a familiar way, sighed like a wretch who had a great weariness to bear on his chest, and warned me, 'When you go to see them, they will ask you questions; be careful what you say to them.' I suspected well enough that I would be asked questions, but I did not see what I could have to hide about myself. I gave him a questioning look. He went on to say, 'I am criticized for giving short sessions. They will try to find out about this from you. It is true that as an experiment, and for short periods, I have shortened sessions with you and with some others who are also coming to an end. It would be in your interests to say nothing about this if you want to be accepted. Besides, you have seen for yourself that this frustration has been useful to you. You have regressed. This has done you immense good.' I had seen nothing of the sort. Everything collapsed around me. Could it be that psychoanalysis was manipulation or trickery? Of my own accord I had my last sessions seated opposite this Wise Man that I wanted to see face to face at last, and whose true measure I wanted to take before giving him his cards. At home, I set about drawing up a written balance sheet of my psychoanalysis—he had asked me, 'justify your wish to end it'—and afterwards I read it out to him. The freedom of speech of which I had availed myself during those four years had succeeded in loosening the internalized grip of my parents' cares and concerns. My fear of an inherited psychopathology had been dispelled. My wife and I had been able to have our first baby with joy and to prepare ourselves to conceive the second. I had successfully presented my first scientific communication to the Société Française de Psychologie on the problems of validating projective tests. I felt less anxious. But there remained my temper outbursts, which had never been analysed. The complexity of my relationship to a maternal image that was split between an ideal mother and a persecuting mother remained untouched. I was only happy intermittently. Thinking about myself more psychoanalytically with the help of Anna Freud's book *The Ego and the Mechanisms of Defence*, which had just come out in French, led me to discover that a whole series of defence mechanisms had lost their virulence and that I had at my disposal a great deal more energy that had thereby been released. Lacan believed that I owed to him this awareness that I had come to *in extremis*. He asked for my notes: he wanted to publish them. In making him the false promise that I would bring them to him when I had got them in order, I had inwardly laughed at him for the first and also for the last time.

I had had a spell of Catholic religious education before I reached puberty. I used then to go to confession. I had learned by trial and error that it was best to pick and choose among what I had to say and how certain deeds or acts needed to be presented and arranged so as not to annoy the priest. I stopped going to confession and lost my religious faith when I realized that confession, absolution, and repentance served no purpose, that the same desires—sexual or aggressive—continued, and that I was falling back into the same 'errors'. I had carried over into psychoanalysis my need to establish a truthful relationship with an interlocutor—and with myself—and here I was up against an analogous disappointment. The bitterness stayed with me until my second analysis, with Georges Favez. His Swiss sturdiness, his great internal availability, his firmness in putting his finger on my errors in understanding myself, and the abundance and pertinence of his interpretations about my early oedipal conflicts freed me from my susceptibilities and resentments, reconciled me in love with my mother, and enabled me to create the various new ideas with which I think I have enriched the psychoanalytic field. While I was waiting, I chose to become a psychologist: I needed to do that in a certain solitary way. The third or fourth version of my autobiography, which was always unfinished, began thus at that time: 'I am an unloved son of unloved parents.' It didn't get much further than these opening words. The general title that I gave it condensed very well my internal situation: *Un psychologue incertain* [An Uncertain Psychologist].

In the meantime, I had proceeded on my new round of training psychoanalysts. When I was asked, I answered that I had had short sessions for a certain period of time. I also let on with what intensity, suffering, and hopes I had experienced my treatment. I was able to tell Princess Marie Bonaparte, who enquired, that I no longer felt guilty about having lost my faith in God, because I had realized that human beings are mortal, body and soul, and that they need to accommodate themselves to this fear and disappointment. I was admitted as a student in 1953, and I began my training by attending Lagache's group supervision seminar, and then by having individual supervision from Juliette Favez-Boutonier.

Freudian psychoanalysis, Lacanian psychoanalysis

G T: Didier Anzieu, you have weighed up your experience with Lacan—in what respects it was analytic despite everything, and where a 'Lacan affair', something that was to break out later on, was present in it in embryo. We will now spend a moment talking about Lacan— not now as an analyst, but about his system of thought. You are known in France as one of the principal representatives of orthodox psychoanalysis. Lacan, with his cliques, is at the diametrically opposite pole. Could you describe, this time in detail, the major and fundamental differences rather than the anecdotal ones (like the fact that some of Lacan's sessions were cut short) between these two systems of thought: yours and Lacan's?

DA: Since you present me as an exponent of orthodoxy, I would first of all like to make it clear on which points I would accept this description and on which I do not really think it fits. I would not hesitate to describe myself as orthodox in the sense in which, like any analyst recognized by the International Psychoanalytic Association, I consider that the patients we take into psychoanalysis in the strict sense of the term (and not into psychotherapy, where the setting is managed differently) must be seen several times a week, three times at least, for sessions of something like forty-five minutes, that the agreed timetable should be respected by the analyst, and that the rule of abstinence is fundamental, abstinence certainly from amorous, sexual, or aggressive relations with the patient, but also from friendly, social, worldly, or business relationships (Lacan, by contrast, liked to ask his patients to do him little favours—to bring a book, to look up the meaning of a foreign word in a dictionary, to contact somebody for him, etc.). We consider that the analyst's essential tool is interpretation, which must be communicated at the appropriate moment, neither too early nor too late, and with restraint, though there might be times when it needs to be prepared gradually beforehand and later repeated in a variety of different ways. . . .

GT: Hermeneutic work, to use Ricoeur's language. . . .

DA: If you like. But twofold interpretative work: in the psychoanalyst, and in the patient. The psychoanalyst takes the initiative so as to get it going in the analysand, who will then do it more and more for himself. For Lacan and his followers—or, rather, his imitators—on the contrary, the analyst's role is reduced to floating attention, which they call 'listening', and to engendering sufficient frustration by means of systematic silence to bring the patient's phantasies to light. But confronted with the latter, the patient is supposed himself to pick out the infantile attitudes they conceal, which he will renounce when he establishes their infantile character—what a utopia!—and also the forbidden desires they contain, which will then turn out to be possible and will transform an individual lost among illusory longings into a subject with desires—and to hell with other people, whose

desires are not compatible with his own! For me, the interpretation that the psychoanalyst offers engages with what
the patient himself makes of varied communications—sometimes stimulating, supportive, alongside him, and sometimes antagonistic, revealing, agonizing, or disillusioning.
What is more, the psychoanalyst does nothing but interpret.
An analysis can include long periods of silence on his part, or
equally on the patient's part. In the latter, silence might
betray a resistance, or a renunciation of superficial chatter
and an approach towards an existential affect that has previously been repressed. Sometimes interpretation can be
prompt. In the first session of a treatment, or with the first
words uttered in a session, the analysand may report a
dream, a remark, or an event the meaning of whose narrative is so obviously transferential that it can elicit an
immediate and unforeseen interpretation that pops out as a
surprise as much to the analyst who hears himself give it as
to the patient who is grabbed by it.

I would like to register my disagreement on two other
points with the Lacanian technique of intepretation. The
principle according to which the unconscious is seen as structured like a language leads the psychoanalyst to 'pinpoint' in
the patient's 'discourse' the key 'signifiers'—those into the
very 'letter' of which unconscious phantasy may have stolen
surreptitiously. When he does give an interpretation, a Lacanian psychoanalyst isolates, decomposes, and recombines a
verbal sequence in order to reveal an unconscious meaning
that the patient was obviously unintentionally revealing in
his word-for-word or even 'letter-for-letter' text, in the manner of a slip of the tongue or a joke. This could in fact be an
occasion for giving a humorous interpretation if the rest of
the clinical material demands it: but it also runs the risk of
being funny at the patient's expense and intruding upon
him. All too often this consists on the psychoanalyst's side—
but should he still be called a psychoanalyst?—in a pure
exercise of linguistic virtuosity. At best he replaces the analysand's word play with his own. At worst, by means of a sort

of intellectual terrorism, he arbitrarily covers over the patient's affective problems with distorting, preconceived knowledge.

The letter as agency, which Lacan makes a fundamental characteristic of the unconscious, itself depends upon word play whose aim is to fuse the two meanings of the word 'letter': a text sent to an absent recipient, and the basic element of the alphabet that makes up written language. It therefore confuses two realities—the code and the message—whose distinction is one of the basic tenets of linguistics. When they do not exhaust the patient, stylistic exercises such as these reinforce his fascinated admiration for the analyst by making him believe that the latter knows everything about him that he himself not only does not know, but will never be able to tell him about except in a cryptic manner and while indefinitely adrift. I have had enough patients in treatment for a second analysis who have been submitted to this régime to know that they did not benefit from it either in terms of developing a psychoanalytic process or in terms of an improvement in their state. All the same, they needed time and courage to resolve to wake up to the fact that on a series of essential problems their psychoanalysis was keeping to a superficial level, and to draw conclusions from this.

GT: You mentioned a second technical disagreement.

DA: This second point flows from another principle. For Lacan, interpretation consists in returning a message to its sender in inverted form. It is a pity that he did not give a single example of this that would have shed light on what he meant by 'inverted form'. Apart from regarding the analyst's obstinate silence as a modality of return that is intended to inform the message's sender that his demand was so infantile and phantasy-laden that he did not even deserve to be told as much. This is a technique employed by masters of Zen Buddhism in the formation of monks. Lacan often reminded one of it. This device, which has nothing to do with psycho-analysis, confirms the analyst in the position of Master, which the patient's unconscious is only too ready to put him in. The model of the mirror stage underlies this theory of interpretation. Lacan borrowed it in 1936 from the child psychologists who had discovered it and transferred it to psychoanalysis. A mirror returns our own image to us in a symmetry that is inverted in the sagittal plane: the left side of our body becomes the right side of our image, and vice versa. But in order actually to perceive himself, the person gazing into a mirror needs to detach himself from his nar-cissistic fascination and infantile jubilation at seeing him-self complete and 'beautiful' for the first time. Conceived of in these terms, psychoanalytic interpretation would betray an active refusal on the analyst's part to function as a complac-ent narcissistic mirror and would instead confront the patient with the structural differences misunderstood by his neurosis, especially those of sex and generation. This approach confuses means and ends; it puts the cart before the horse. If it is indeed the ultimate aim of psychoanalytic treatment to free the patient from his narcissistic illusions and to restructure his psychic functioning around the oedipal problematic, then the way ahead is not through the analyst imposing himself upon him. What is required is lengthy and sustained work, analysing the patient's narcissistic flaws and injuries, their nature, their probable origins, the hyper-cathexes that have come along to block them up and hide them, the frequent splitting between idealization and per-secution, the confusion between what belongs to self and what has been done by others, and so on. Premature denun-ciation of narcissistic deficiencies can open the way not to the necessary journey through depression, but to a useless and dangerous decompensation. Access to the difference between the sexes and generations, which is in fact fundamental, often turns out to have been obstructed and complicated by uncertainties that can also be resolved by means of work that is equally meticulous about the most primary distinctions between animate and inanimate, external and internal reality, dreams and waking, and so on.

GT: Your conception of interpretation is effectively classical. On what points do you hold less orthodox positions?

DA: If, as Lacan maintained, there is no psychoanalysis without constant reference back to Freud (and implicitly to Lacan as Freud's Number One exegete), then I feel I am much less orthodox. Freud certainly made an exceptional discovery. Between the ages of forty and eighty he was constantly bringing to light new sets of information about the unconscious; he connected them into a vast global theory that was itself in evolution; he launched an organization whose task was to transmit psychoanalysis, to ensure the training of psychoanalysts, and to monitor the quality and rigour of their practice—preconditions for the success of treatment. His great stature fills the scene, and there is no need to address a religious cult to his work, which speaks for itself. Many of his companions and successors became creative as a result of self-analysis, on Freud's model, or through their personal psychoanalysis. Karl Abraham with ambivalence, Ferenczi with projection, and Jones with symbolism originated clinical and theoretical progress, which Freud took up. Psychoanalytic work that produces discoveries complementary to Freud's has flourished in the past and is still flourishing today. Some discoveries even bring the Master's views into question and make it necessary to rethink entire areas of clinical work, theory, and technique. In England, Melanie Klein extended psychoanalysis to young children and psychotics. Her disciple Bion took it into groups. There was a heated and lasting dispute between Melanie Klein and Anna Freud, Sigmund's daughter—in other words, between defenders of a wide orthodoxy and partisans of a narrow orthodoxy. Several of the English psychoanalysts who kept themselves out of this dispute, while from time to time deriving something useful from one side or the other, furnished new ideas that are accepted today: Balint with the basic fault, or Winnicott with transitional phenomena. More recently, the psychoanalytic approach to patients who are neither neurotic nor psychotic—they are described as narcissistic or borderline personalities, and they have become our most numerous patients in psychoanalysis—has caused an upheaval in our conceptions of transference and the structure of the ego. Here I am thinking, for example, of the work of Kohut and Kernberg in the United States. There is no longer one single psychoanalytic theory, any more than there is a single uniform theory in modern physics. There are psychoanalytic theories in the plural—each more appropriate for a certain type of patient or even analyst, or for a particular moment in treatment. Psychic functioning is of a variety and richness (and sometimes poverty) that defies all classification, and all systematized structural explanation. The psychic Self increasingly appears to be composed of disparate pieces; some are distinct and coherent, or different but still tending to agglutinate; others are felt to be strangers by the ego; still others are deported and encapsulated on the periphery of the mind, where they constitute a hidden Self, a silent source of depression. The same disparity is found in references to theory. Each psychoanalyst, depending upon his personality, style, experience, and patient, turns to more or less diverse bits of psychoanalytic theory that give him something to hold onto—make no mistake about it—a symbolic warrant for his psychic work of understanding and his psychoanalytic work of interpretation. Psychoanalytic orthodoxy resides and subsists only in technique: Lacan was deficient in this with his short sessions, the extra-psychoanalytic contacts that he had with patients, and his silence instead of interpretation. By contrast, it is more difficult to uphold the idea of orthodoxy in the domain of theory on account of the questioning and renewal of concepts. For my part—but we shall no doubt have the opportunity to return to this, since it risks taking us away from Lacan—I attach great importance to the body and to the biological roots of the mind—to the relations between the psychic Ego and the body Ego, their respective boundaries and fluctuations in the latter, and to all the material of primary sensations that are subsequently articulated with the drives and organized into phantasies and conflicts.

GT: We will return to this later, because you have built up a theory around this relationship between body and mind, but let us stay with Jacques Lacan. You have described in which respects you were orthodox and in which you were less so. In all this, where did Lacan and his system of thought diverge fundamentally from your own?

DA: It is difficult with Lacan to distinguish his personal style from the theoretical views that he put forward. In my reaction, which was progressively one of disillusionment, then detachment,and finally opposition to him—in my reaction, then, Lacan the person and Lacan's ideas are intermingled. I can only make rather artificial distinctions between them. I will now try to explain myself. Once the analysis was ended, Lacan continued to exert an influence over his former patients, who had now become pupils.

GT: Would you say that he dominated them?

DA: What I would say is this: having failed to dissolve the transference because he had minimized the negative transference, analysis of which would have allowed patients to detach themselves from their analyst and the analyst to detach himself from his patients—having thus attempted to sidestep the negative transference, and having instead adopted the attitude I have mentioned of a good, warm, amicable, and obliging relationship on the periphery of sessions—Lacan displaced and prolonged the treatment transference into his seminar. Once treatment was ended, and even before, one started attending Lacan's seminar, and one left treatment in order to attend it for the rest of one's life, indefinitely. One evening in 1953, between the first split (that happened in the Société Psychanalytique de Paris) and the creation of the Société Française de Psychanalyse, Lacan gathered his pupils together in the basement of the Café Capoulade on the corner of the rue Soufflot and the boulevard Saint-Michel. He gave a little speech about his joy that a new society was about to be founded. At last he was going to be able to develop his ideas. And he ended his harangue with, 'Follow me, I will lead you to the ends of the earth'.

GT: Just like Moreno, I think.

DA: It was in fact much the same sort of thing. But Lacan did it in a more muted and less overtly theatrical way. This expression astonished me, because I could not see how a man—even an analyst—could lead other people to the ends of the earth. And the seminar was just like that. One was kept on tenterhooks and driven back upon one's own ignorance. He alone knew, without deigning to share his knowledge: 'I will explain next time', he would say. Or, again, 'I am going to write a book that will account for what I am doing' . . . and then Lacan never wrote a book (aside from his medical thesis on paranoia); he contented himself with letting his son-in-law assemble his *Writings*. One never got an answer to questions like what justification there was for short sessions, or what difference he was introducing between a signifier as he undestood it and the same concept as used in linguistic terminology. The seminar was spellbinding because three illusions were at work together: the unconscious, or so one was led to think, was speaking there in a necessarily obscure way through the mouthpiece of him who was its master; there was a chance that the interpretation that had been refused during sessions might be given in public, and it sometimes was; and there was the promise that new words would infuse the hackneyed notions of the psychoanalytic tribe with a purer meaning.

GT: Readers should be reminded that Lacan's whole thesis is ultimately founded on the conception that the unconscious is structured in the same way as language itself is structured. The unconscious is seen as coded, on the same model that maintains that speech is organized by the linguistic code. . . .

DA: Absolutely.

GT: Well, do you find this idea interesting at that level? Could you give me your opinion about it?

DA: The statement that he gradually focussed upon (namely that the unconscious is structured *like* a language—a prudent formulation, since this 'like' leaves the door open for many analogies), if we take this statement as a scientific one, it can neither be proved nor refuted, since by definition, of its very essence, the unconscious eludes knowledge founded upon verbal thought. I cannot say whether I agree or disagree with this statement, since I know nothing about it, and nothing can be known about it. Lacan wanted to detach psychoanalysis from American influence, which would make it into a branch of psychiatry, behaviourism, and even neuro-physiology of the brain (Freud started out from the latter beginning). Lacan tried to re-situate psychoanalysis within one of the essential areas opened up by Freud, namely within the world of culture, together with the unconscious substructure included in culture, which Freud brought clearly to light. The considerable development of the human and social sciences soon after the Second World War, and also of anthropology, provided the latter is taken in the broad sense and not reduced to ethnology, gave Lacan the idea of a rapprochement with the anthropology of Lévi-Strauss, the linguistics of Jakobson, and the structuralism subsequently developed by Barthes. Lacan reminded us that the qualities necessary for a psychoanalyst are every bit as much the products of a training in literature, philosophy, and anthropology as one in medicine, neuro-biology, and psychiatry. Here he was absolutely right, and this explains why, after having ended my psychoanalysis with him, I continued for several years to attend his classes, in a position that was admittedly ever more marginal and which allowed me to escape more quickly than many of my contemporaries from the interminable dependency into which he was drawing his pupils. We were able to re-read Freud in an interesting way within the Lacanian perspective: to establish, for example, that the cathartic method under hypnosis was verbal chimney-sweeping; to notice, on going back to the first published cases in the *Studies on Hysteria* or *The Interpretation of Dreams*, that plenty of examples of stammering, nervous coughs, and other forms of attack on speech are to be found there, that there are cases of forgetting the mother tongue, and cases of discourse in foreign languages: that here, in fact, was a whole collection of material about language that Freud never theorized nor systematized, but which is effectively present in many of his observations. Having said this, I myself (and this is both what makes me opposed to Lacan and makes me think that I am profoundly Freudian while at the same time being only moderately orthodox with respect to hegemonic psychoanalytic theories)—I myself would oppose the formula: 'the unconscious is structured like a language' with a formulation that is implicit in Freud: 'the unconscious is the body'. The unconscious seems to me to be structured like the body—not the body as studied and represented by anatomo-physiologists, but the body of the phantastic anatomy of hysteria and infantile sexual theories (as Freud clearly showed); and, more fundamentally still, in a more primary and archaic manner, the body as source of the first sensory-motor experiences, the first communications, and the oppositions that relate to the very basis of perception and thought.

GT: We will return to that, for we have not finished with Lacan. Lacan also gave rise to the phenomenon of Lacanism, and different Lacanian schools. Without wishing to make this dialogue between ourselves into a sort of coffee-table discussion or a collection of anecdotes that have gone the rounds or turn upon the Lacan phenomenon, it is nonetheless a fact that these Lacanian cliques have given rise to various scandals. For example, it seems that towards the end of his life Lacan had great difficulty in giving a talk, in actually articulating, and that the texts that he was scarcely able to read out had been written in pure Lacanian style by his son-in-law Jacques-Alain Miller. However that may be, it is a fact that Lacanism has been very important in psychoanalytic thinking in France, and even internationally: the Americans have taken an interest in it, and Lacan has already been translated into English (by the Americans, who are usually very isolationist, so it is a rare tribute, when one thinks how Piaget was only discovered there some twenty years ago, and how Lévi-Strauss was not translated in the United States until very late in the day). The fact that Lacan is beginning to penetrate over there is not a proof in itself, but it does mean all the same that the phenomenon is not confined to France but has crossed its borders. How is that to be interpreted? That is my first question. Can one explain the success of Lacanism in terms of a phenomenon of fashion: that since orthodox psychoanalysis was tired, something else had to be found? Or does this success rest upon more important and richer foundations? My second question is, therefore, as follows: Lacanism is not, after all, Lacan. Can one differentiate Lacan's original contribution from the use that his disciples have subsequently made of it?

DA: First of all, so far as the end of Lacan's life is concerned, I had broken with him a very long time beforehand. I no longer had any personal contact with him at that time. Like you, I have heard the rumours that you mention, but I cannot offer any opinion about them. For my part, I deplore the way in which, when a man becomes old and ill—a fate that lies in store for all of us—people take advantage of his weakness to pounce upon him: that disgusts me. I criticized Lacan when he was strong, capable of defending himself, and capable of replying. I refused all polemics starting the moment he was personally afflicted. He had to be allowed to end his life in dignity. His approaching death affected his relationship with himself, his own, and his family. It no longer concerned the rest. I find it obscene that disciples who paid allegiance to him so long as they could feed at his seminar should wait until he was without strength and speechless to change their colours, to attack him, decide to reject him and go to form other groups. Whatever my theoretical and personal disagreements with this man, he was a man. And, like any man, he deserved to be treated with respect when he was suffering and dying. That is one reason why I refused to write or speak about him just after his death. I made a point of it.

GT: Why has Lacanism been so successful?

DA: After Freud's death, the other psychoanalytic societies in France and in most countries were organized in a manner . . . the words that come to me are clumsy, but let us say: that was more or less democratic or self-governing, and in which confirmed analysts regarded themselves as being on an equal footing with one another: I am referring to those who were responsible for the training of young analysts. Perhaps one had more talent for writing, another was better at speaking, a third might be more successful with a particular type of patient, but they all regarded one another as peers: none of them asserted pre-eminence. This had been accepted and wished for by Freud himself. Had he not always refused presidency of the International Psychoanalytic Association? Melanie Klein stirred up enormous controversial discussions in so far as she proposed a rather different theoretical system and made very vigorous and rigorous efforts to get Kleinian orthodoxy respected, and it took the solid, centuries-old empiricist tradition of the English to prevent

their psychoanalytic society from splitting apart. In France
for a long time there were four psychoanalytic societies
(there are more at present, but before Lacan's death there
were only four). Three of them were run on the collegiate
principle of equality among members. The fourth was
organized by a director who got himself voted in for five years
and was renewable in perpetuity—you have spotted
Lacan—in other words, on the principle of a master in thinking who took it upon himself to think for others. It is no
accident that this group called itself a 'school': l'École Freudienne de Paris. This was one of my additional reasons for
breaking with it. For me, there are no masters in thinking. I
do not mean that someone like Lévi-Strauss does not know
more, in ethnology, than many specialists, but he never
imposed himself as a master in thinking. He said, more or
less; 'I have a method, which is structural; I apply it systematically in order to see just how far one can go with it in
anthropology, taking it as far as possible. When it won't go
any further, people will need to resort to another method,
and in this way the limits of mine will become known.' He
never claimed to explain everything with it. What is more,
he patently refrained from extrapolating his method and
discoveries into a field other than that of 'savages', who were
his particular clinical domain. There are individuals who
encourage us to think, and who help us to make discoveries,
but there cannot exist a unique master in thinking who
definitively thinks in our stead. There are masters in the
plural, various and provisional. I have myself mentioned
those who contributed to my formation, for whom I retain
affection and esteem, and in relation to whom I have sooner
or later had to make allowances and to distance myself. I
have been able to criticize them and to recognize their limita-
tions and blind spots, while knowing what a debt I owe them.

Lacan put himself forward and imposed himself as a life-
long master. In *Group Psychology and the Analysis of the Ego*
Freud described the idealization of a chief and the idea he is
bearer of, the collective quasi-hypnotic identification that

follows from that, and the rejection of aggression outside the group that is unified in this way. Lacan, partly out of his natural narcissism and partly through calculation and sharp practice, got these processes going within the psychoanalytic school that he founded. There is no need to be surprised at his success, which rests upon a skilful exploitation of the laws of the psychology of a group's unconscious. On the other hand one should be amazed that an analyst, instead of analysing these phenomena when they arise, as Freud pointed the way towards doing, preferred to tap them to his own advantage. Lacan kept his pupils in the role of interminable disciples and his patients in the role of interminable analys-ands. His seminar was interminable. And woe betide those who kicked against the pricks. They were flogged in public (verbally, of course), brought back to heel, and threatened with finding themselves deprived of a practice or driven out in disgrace and humiliation.

GT: All this because of the negative transference you were talking about a little while ago. But this does not explain the success of Lacanism outside France, for example in Italy, Spain, Portugal, South America, and Quebec: one finds people everywhere who claim to be Lacanians and who have been trained, not necessarily by Lacan himself, but by one of his disciples, and who spread his 'good news' around the world.

DA: By declaring that a psychoanalyst could only be authorized by himself, Lacan facilitated recruitment to his school. Many people were thus entitled psychoanalysts while sidestepping the stages of selection and training, and instead holding Lacanian conversations as their guarantee. There was no formation outside contact with Lacan. And in place of the missing training there was servitude. Contrary to what one might think, the offer of servitude could pay off. Neurosis needs a master; our masochism cries out for an executioner; our narcissism makes us search for a double who can reflect an ideal image to us; and the individual who believes himself to be castrated seeks out a phallus to cut down or else to worship. These statements are part of the universal message of psychoanalysis. Even if it knows that it will never make them disappear, it analyses these needs, unpacks them, elucidates them, and works towards their relief. The message of Lacanism is universal in another sense. It panders to this need while appearing to denounce it. It illustrates this manoeuvre by setting the psychoanalyst up as a supposedly absolute prince in order to reflect to the patient or student, with irony and derision, that figure of a prince that each of us unconsciously bears within ourselves, and that need for voluntary servitude so well described by La Boétie. The Lacanian psychoanalyst takes such delight in this game that here he is actually becoming a prince, or a delegate of a prince in a quarter of the universe in which he reproduces over others the domination that he submitted to in his own Lacanian psychoanalysis. Lacan held his pupils in such contempt that he actually told them in his seminar that he himself, who embodied the figure of the prince for their unconscious, was deliberately responding to their need by behaving as a prince towards them, and that they were letting themselves be trapped into it. That is the language of Machiavelli. It is not that of Freud, despite the return to the founding father of psychoanalysis that the Lacanians go on about in order all the better to disguise their 'Machiavellian' intentions. Here we have a distortion of psychoanalysis and its ethics. We should not be surprised that Machiavellianism is effective. But it is only effective for a time, until it becomes too obvious, too unbearable, and turns back against its exponents.

GT: It seems to me that this was indeed part of Lacan's method. But that was analysed. He pushed his patients into analysing this relationship to the prince. And this need that they had for a prince was also a way of pointing towards their potential freedom from delusion. When faced with an attitude like that, there is always a way of extricating oneself from it. In the end the analyst can say that he had acted in this way for their own good.

DA: The ones who extricated themselves did so by slamming the door and going to found, in turn, the Association Psychanalytique de France in 1962, then the Quatrième group, and finally some of the sub-groups that have formed themselves recently. Lacan stuck to a language that was paradoxical in the sense in which the school of Palo Alto has developed the theory of the paradox and demonstrated its pathogenic power. At the same time as he was telling his pupils that the figure of the prince was inside them and that they therefore had to become aware of it, he remained the all-powerful director: he remained the central figure in his seminars, and he contradicted his doctrine with his behaviour. As soon as one of his students showed a little sparkle and claimed to interpret Lacan's thinking, to fill it out or rectify it, he became the favourite target of the master, who let fly his arrows at him. To take an example: when in 1960, at the Colloque de Bonneval on the unconscious, Jean Laplanche and Serge Leclaire gave their paper in which they maintained that it was language that was structured like the unconscious and not the unconscious that was structured like a language, Lacan did not forgive them. Laplanche drew the consequences of this by associating himself, as I did, with the Committee that went on to found the Association Psychanalytique de France. Leclaire became a marginal figure, who never succeeded either in completely resigning or in making a place for himself within the École Freudienne de Paris.

GT: This still does not explain Lacan's success.

DA: That is true. Power only comes to those who desire it strongly and know how to handle collective psychology skilfully in order to get it. One would have thought that in a psychoanalyst his phantasy relationship with power, his desire for narcissistic omnipotence, his fascination with the dialectic of master and slave, and his propensity to behave as a strategist because it is easier and more advantageous in managing conflicts with others than to speak truthfully— one would have thought that these tendencies, marked as they are with the stamp of pregenitality, would have been sufficiently analysed and decathected. One would likewise have thought that a psychoanalyst would have quickly learned by experience that the prolonged and solitary exercise of power makes one a persecutor (and persecuted), and that the more absolute power is, the more its wielder tends to except himself from common law, to pander to his passions, to unleash his madness, and to reincarnate that image of the father of the primitive horde, omnipotent, egotistical, and cruel, who was described so well by Freud. But something else is also needed: this man, who idealizes himself and demands to be idealized, must put ideas forward. Lacan never lacked ideas, even if he rarely cited his sources when they were ideas 'borrowed' from others and even if, in order to increase 'suspense', he was tacitly twisting the meaning of an everyday word or concept in philosophy or linguistics. Lacan put a host of ideas into circulation that not only interested analysts, but professors of Letters or Philosophy, Jesuits and Dominicans, professional writers and thinkers, and a whole world badly in need of new words in the absence of accurate thoughts. He got debate going again, he encouraged stylistic research in writing, he rejuvenated the figures and tropes of old rhetoric by drawing a parallel between them and unconscious defence mechanisms, and he had hopes that it would be possible to formalize the logic of the primary psychic processes. Here is a list of his ideas, without claiming either that they are in any particular order or that they are exhaustive: the mirror stage; the distinction between the three registers of the imaginary, the symbolic, and the real; the other distinction between desire, need, and demand; the role of the signifier in the articulation of phantasy and discourse, and the endless parade of signifiers; the splitting of the subject; the name of the father and its fore-

closure in psychosis; how unconscious formations are produced by metaphorical and metonymic processes; deep-
seated alienation through displacement into the Other's
place; the human being [*être humain*] as a speaking being
[*parlêtre*], which structures itself by means of language
[*lalangue*, in a single word], etc. One could write—and,
indeed, books have been written—about each of his ideas.
Unfortunately, mixing in Lacanian circles, familiarity with
these notions, and facility in playing with them in conversation and making them glitter with myriad lights, have done
little to help Lacan's followers to acquire a clinical sense and
to work psychoanalytically with their patients. These ideas
do not stand up well to the test of clinical practice. Thus,
when I began psychoanalytic practice with and thinking
about groups, I started off with the Lacanian distinction
between the imaginary, the symbolic, and the real. But I had
to abandon it after some years of vain effort because it only
provided me with a superficial description of the phenomena.
I owe it to my reading of Melanie Klein and then Bion that
my mind has been opened up to the levels of anxiety and the
different types of phantasy that are mobilized in group situations.

GT: Perhaps we could stop a moment, without going into
too many details, over the Lacanian concept of the fourth
dimension that he spoke about: the phantasy of God. What do
you think about it? In fact the key, the very basis of Lacan's
Writings, turns on this fourth term, which is essential with
Lacan in order to escape classical oedipal triangulation. For
Lacan, the impossible fulfils this function even more than
does the real. Could we have your opinion about this?

DA: I am going to give you my own personal convictions
first of all, because I think that one should always make clear
one's personal conviction before criticizing that of others, so
that the reader can make allowances for the possible role of
one's own belief in the judgement that one is making about

someone else's. I believe in the non-existence of God and in the mortality of the soul as much as of the body. Having said that, through analytic neutrality, through deep-seated liberalism, and also because I know what positive elements I have preserved from the moral and religious education I received, I respect the religious, philosophical, artistic, and political beliefs not only of my patients but of every individual. It goes without saying that a psychoanalyst does not busy himself with these matters in the treatment he offers, and that he leaves his patients free to maintain their beliefs or to abandon them if they become aware of the neurotic roots of their attachment to them. Like Freud, I am a materialist. Like him, I consider religion, art, and philosophy as illusions, but necessary illusions. Human beings need ideals, and the earliest traces of a religious cult—the palaeolithic drawings on the walls of caves—testify to the emergence of the superego, decisive in the processes of hominization and civilization.

In a context in which the ethics of psychoanalysis is suffering increasingly serious and frequent infringements at the hands of certain practitioners, it seems to me essential to remember that the aims of psychoanalysis cannot be reduced either to the liberation of repressed wishes nor to the decentring of psychic functioning in relation to a calculating and defensive preconscious or unconscious ego, but that they include diminution of narcissistic ideas of omnipotence, domination, and seduction, and giving a larger and more secure place to ideals of shared happiness, liberty, justice, and attention to others. What seemed curious to me about Lacan was that at the same time as he was propagating topics like those that I have mentioned, he still implied that the unconscious as he conceived it—that is, structured like a language—was not unrelated to that sacred beginning which, according to St. John's Gospel, was the Word before it became flesh. Or again, commenting upon what Pascal called the hidden God, he implied that the unconscious must be this hidden God that we have in us—whence, what is more, the fascination that Lacanism has had for certain Catholics who, despite the repeated condemnation of psychoanalysis by various Popes, have been eager to make religion compatible with the findings of the human and social sciences.

One difference between the human and natural sciences is that in the latter, when a discovery is made, it is accepted after verification and discussion until a new discovery leads to rethinking it and resituating it differently within a new theory. Nothing, by contrast, is ever established in the human sciences because the fear of death, the desire for eternity, the dream of absolute power, and many more expedients besides that are linked with archaic psychic processes keep cropping up repeatedly, no matter what scientific, pedagogic, or political systems have actually been developed. From this point of view, Lacanism is an illustration of a general phenomenon, and Lacan played, I think, altogether skilfully and consciously upon this ambiguity between a religious message and the language of the contemporary human sciences.

GT: He manoeuvred well?

DA: The word 'maneouvre' seems too crude. . . .

GT: Let us say then that he was a good strategist, if you prefer.

DA: Yes, I prefer that term. Lacan did have a strategy, while other analysts only had tactics. There are a few of us who followed Lacan with interest, even with enthusiasm, so long as he was unknown outside a circle of analysts, doctors, and philosophers. Once he had acquired this base (and I say base in the military sense of the term), Lacan set out on the conquest of the cultural milieu. This was a deliberate intention on his part, a strategic design; from that point on, he deployed various series of local and specific tactics, which allowed him to achieve this result. He gradually became a figure talked about in the mass media, and he systematically cultivated his stardom. For me, one cannot remain an analyst if one becomes a public figure. Certainly, analysts defend and promote analysis, they make it known, they publish their work, and they debate with specialists in adjacent disciplines, but it is inconceivable that they should pose as stars.

GT: All the same, M Anzieu, the question one might ask oneself at this point is the following: 'Can one be a strategist, or can one occupy a cultural territory without there being meat on the product one wants to sell?' Now there seems to have been plenty of meat where Lacan is concerned.

DA: It remains to be seen what sort of meat this was. Lacan's seminar was a spectacle that many have sought in vain to imitate. They would have had to be able to do what he did: for example, to stand there speaking for two hours without notes, being 'inspired'. I never attended an inspired sermon during the short religious period of my life, but I imagine inspired speeches like this were made among the early Christians or among the Quakers when they landed in the United States. Here again we find the kinship between Lacanism and religious experience: or, if you prefer, spectator society. His youthful experience with the surrealists certainly helped him. He undoubtedly also had gifts, a facility for casting loose from his moorings and letting free associations run on, verbally as well as at a level of deeper images.

GT: We must not forget that Lacan was also a theatrical man. . . .

DA: There was a whole performance in his seminars. Even if he had prepared a text, he was capable of departing from it: one would witness how a new idea would come to him all of a sudden, and how he would himself be dazzled by the idea and set about playing with it.

GT: This was improvisation, ultimately. . . .

DA: Sometimes there was improvisation on his part, and sometimes he calculated his effects.

GT: But this seems to have answered to a need. People in fact adore watching someone improvise, be dazzled by his own findings, his own products, and play with them like that before a public. It must also be said that he did not play any old how—he played well.

DA: I have an answer to your question about why things went so well with him. It is because he played very well. If the audience was spellbound, it is because they asked for nothing else. So, my dear M Tarrab, we have gone back to a century ago, to a date in the history of medicine and psychology before the discovery of psychoanalysis: we have gone back quite simply to suggestion and hypnosis.

GT: We could talk about that, despite the fact that Freud rejected it as a therapeutic technique; none the less today hypnosis is being talked about afresh.

DA: I am not against it if it is used to treat the sick individually. So far as therapeutic approaches are concerned, I insist upon a certain eclecticism: with each case one must find the technique that will suit it best. I tend to point various patients who consult me in different directions, towards a form of brief therapy, towards psychodrama, towards relaxation, or hypnosis, or group dynamics, and not necessarily towards psychoanalysis. But in his seminar, Lacan was dealing with pupils who wanted to become psychoanalysts and to be trained as such. I say that in this case hypnosis is not a good method of formation. I hold that the hypnotic relationship, an amorous relationship, and the relationship of a prince to his vassals are not appropriate relationships for training analysts.

GT: You have touched there on several things. But to finish with Lacan, I would like to quote from this little-known text that Lacan delivered on the occasion of one of his seminars on 'love': 'If psychoanalysis is a means, it stands *in the place* that love stands in [. . .]. In reality, love becomes the means by which death is united with enjoyment.' Following on from this, what are we to make of being in love, which is generally regarded as a regression by orthodox psycho-analysts, as I recall? 'Falling in love', as we say in Quebec where I live, would therefore be a regression. On another subject, it seems to me that you and Lacan have many points in common. Both of you are eclectics. Lacan mixed with surrealism, you yourself have taken an interest in it, and you have written on poets and painters. You are also attracted by the theatre. . . .

DA: Absolutely.

GT: There is therefore this element in common between the two of you, which you deal with in different ways. But you do the same work fundamentally: you interpret desire.

DA: Here I must explain myself. Certainly I interpret desire. But I am now going to utter another word that hor-rified Lacan, and one can understand why: and that is the ego. He never stopped trying to demolish the ego as an alienating and falsifying concept, starting with the analysis he made of the mirror stage. To him, the ego [French *Moi*, 'me'] seemed to obstruct the assumption of 'I' [French *Je*], which could not happen unless it was carried by desire and carried desire. Now, I find that the patients who come to seek us out are not only suffering from repression, denial, intellec-tualization, or the projection of their desires, but they also suffer, and sometimes above all, from inadequacies in their ego. The analytic work that I perform therefore bears upon the restoration of their narcissistic security, upon the recon-struction of the early impingements that have handicapped

certain of their mental functions, upon their internal difficulties in cathecting their vigilance and directing their
attention more effectively; in brief, upon the flaws in their
ego and the poor fit among the psychic envelopes that delimit
their self. The Lacanian objective of *realizing desire* is no
longer enough. What a fine programme for a patient who
does not feel desires! When loving and sexual cathexes are
reduced and the temptation for self-destruction predomi-
nates, one risks, by applying this formula to the letter (something that has unfortunately happened several times),
giving free rein not to joyful and fruitful desire as much at
the level of the flesh as of psychic life, but to attacks against
the organs of the body, against the equipment of thought,
and against the patient's own life. The door is open for the
patient to realize the desire to destroy himself if the analyst
is content with stating that only desire matters, regardless of
its nature, and if he does not take into account the relations
between the quality and intensity of desires on the one hand,
and the levels of the ego's organization on the other.

GT: Would you say, where Lacan is concerned, that one
could speak of the liberation of savage desire?

DA: I think he got that from surrealism.

GT: That sort of taste for unconditional and ultimately
uncontrolled liberation of libido? And it is this that you find
dangerous in the Lacanian approach . . . even if the word
'dangerous' is probably too strong. . . .

DA: I would like to put something straight. In the case of
neurosis, analysis has a twofold aim—and here I follow
Georges Favez: to bring about the satisfaction of desire
where that is possible, and its renunciation where that is
necessary. In the case of borderline patients the problems are
different. Renunciation is impossible, because there has
been early deficiency and because inhibition remains mas-

sive. What one finds is blocked is not so advanced as desire. What is perpetually under threat is the feeling of continuity of being, the confidence of inhabiting one's own body, and the boundary between me and not-me. Instead of the fullness of living and desiring, the anguish of emptiness has become central. The strength inherent in desires can no longer be channelled, preserved, and concentrated in activities that are sources of enjoyment. Libidinal but also aggressive energy escapes through holes in an insufficiently formed psychic envelope. There is a constant bleeding away of drives and a permanent impression of a life that is shrunken and in slow motion. Satisfaction is sought from time to time, but at the cost of forcing it with the help of alcohol, drugs, or a male or female prostitute. These act as artificial substitutes for a faltering psychic function and yield satisfaction that does not really give enjoyment, or, if it does so, it is pleasure surpassed by the bitter joy of self-destruction. The death instinct tends to predominate within psychic functioning where the ego remains too partially developed. It can also have its orgasm, of a different quality from the enjoyment shared between two beings who feel both sensuality and tenderness for one another, an orgasm that—temporarily—quells the state of need of the drug addict and makes death seem sweet to a suicide. A little while back you read out a quotation from Lacan who considered—or, rather, deconsidered—love as 'means by which death is united with enjoyment'. This is only true for the types of case I have just been describing. Lacan's theory draws upon a certain number of accurate intuitions but places them wrongly, because it constantly confuses two types of patient: neurotics and borderline patients.

Let me add one more idea. It is necessary to analyse borderline states, with their own particular problematic and flaws, but it is not easily done. It is less easily done than analysing the simple conjunction between defences and desires in the neurotic phantasy that underlies a conflict, together with the compromise formations that stem from them. Borderline states require much more sustained interpretative work.

GT: This makes it all the more necessary for a psychoanalyst to follow Freud's advice to have more analysis himself at the appropriate moment.

DA: Yes, indeed. Meanwhile, every serious analyst should carry out self-analytic work upon himself, take the trouble to discuss his practice with his colleagues, and be aware of his countertransference, while his exchanges with others should sustain this self-analytic trend and the vitality of his psychoanalytic thinking. Now, where Lacan was concerned, this work, which forms a good part of an analyst's formation, was excluded. From the moment when he took a pupil into analysis, this analysis was deemed to be sufficient, even if it had to be interminable. It continued afterwards by attendance at his seminar, so it had all the time to be pursued with him. Experience shows that if a patient has to have further analysis, he can obviously resume with his first analyst, for instance for a limited number of sessions, and get benefit from it. But in general it turns out to be better to approach someone different. Each analyst has his own personality, his own sensitivity, his own theory, and his own way of talking: it is better to have a new analytic experience that is different and has more chance of touching what could not be touched in a first 'slab'. A patient must end up by doing without his analyst. The analyst must forego knowing what becomes of his analysand. It is someone else who will eventually know that, but not necessarily himself. I want to emphasize this additional point of disagreement with Lacan.

The body

G T: M Anzieu, classical psychoanalysts have taken little interest in the real body, which has been scotomized and put between parentheses. At most the notion of body image is acknowledged, while it is absent from Laplanche and Pontalis's *The Language of Psycho-Analysis*. There is a tendency in psychoanalysis to sidestep the body in order to listen to words, above all. You are in this sense unorthodox, since you are one of the rather few classical psychoanalysts who increasingly listen in to bodily vibrations. Could you talk to us about this?

DA: Let's not be unfair. Someone like Sami-Ali, to whom I owe a great deal, did not entitle one of his books *Corps réel, corps imaginaire* [Real body, imaginary body] (Dunod, 1972) by accident. The body is the bedrock of the mind. This is not only for familiar reasons relating to the nervous system: it is obvious that without a cortex there would be no thought. But much more, as Freud guessed and as we can now systematize it, for the following reason: psychic functions, psychic organs, and psychic agencies spring from a concrete basis in organic functioning. For example: identification is the transposition into the psychic domain of the incorporation of food, and in the first instance of the milk given by the mother's breast or feeding bottle. Moral control over thoughts forms on the basis of sphincter control over the faeces. For the moment I am no more than repeating Freudian tenets. Certain character traits make one and the same mark upon the body and the spirit, and Wilhelm Reich, before becoming a dissident of psychoanalysis and originating bio-energy, described extremely well, alongside unconscious psychic resistances, a physical resistance that he called the 'muscular cuirass'. It is to the forefront in certain patients.

GT: By contrast, his theory of orgone and fluids has been rejected. . . .

DA: Because that theory is purely imaginary. To continue, I would say that for me it is not only psychic functions and character traits that are based upon the body, but in fact the psychic agencies themselves: we know that Freud represented the psyche as a system of systems. . . .

GT: As a meta-system. . . .

DA: That's it. Theories that represent the psyche as a system full stop are in error at their very foundations. The psyche is a system that integrates several sub-systems, like the body, which is a collection of several sub-systems. The same goes for the nervous system. Let us take the example of the best-known of these psychic sub-systems. In *The Ego and the Id* Freud wrote in an elliptical way that the superego derives from acoustic roots: this means that the orders, injunctions, and threats that the child has heard uttered are at the origin of the superego—in short, parental voices. It is uncertain whether the unconscious is structured like a language. By contrast, this structuring is more certain for the superego. My wife, who has treated many children with language problems, has clearly emphasized this: the child learns not only words, but rules. Speaking means putting sounds and then words into a certain order that makes them take on a meaning. Language combines a great diversity of phonological, grammatical, lexical, and syntactical rules, so here, too, there is a system of sub-systems. The superego derives from an acoustic origin: it forms with the acquisition of speech. And now where does the ego come from? What is it based upon? Freud said it in a short sentence that was commented upon in a note in *The Ego and the Id* and bears upon the surface of the body. The surface of the body allows us to distinguish excitations of external origin from those of internal origin; just as one of the capital functions of the ego is to distinguish between what belongs to me myself and what does not belong, between what comes from me and the desires, thoughts, and affects of others, and between a physical (the world) or biological (the body) reality outside the mind; the ego is the projection in the psyche of the surface of the body, namely the skin, which makes up this sheet or interface, to speak in modern scientific terms. In fact, tactile experience has the peculiarity in comparison with all other sensory experiences of being at once endogenous and exogenous, active and passive. I touch my nose with my finger: my finger gives me the active sensation of touching something, and my nose gives me the passive sensation of being touched by something. This double sensation, passive and active, is peculiar to the skin. Tactile sensation procures the basic distinction between 'inside' and 'outside', and it is the only one that can provide it; the other senses can only do it by reference to tactile sensation and in complementarity with it and with the formation of this interface. A proof, what is more, is that you find human beings who suffer from blindness or deafness or no sense of smell, and this does not prevent them from living, nor from succeeding in communicating, perhaps in a somewhat more complicated way, but they do communicate. By contrast, there is no human being without a virtually complete envelope of skin. If one seventh of the skin is destroyed by accident, lesion, or burns, the human being dies. One can find a symbolic mode of communication even with a child who was both deaf and blind at birth, starting from increasingly differentiated tactile contacts. The skin is so fundamental, its functioning is taken so much for granted, that no one notices its existence until the moment it fails. . . .

GT: It is acquired knowledge.

DA: It takes a whole effort of reflection to appreciate that this surface is there. Where does it come from, what are its functions, what role does it play, what are its excesses, its flaws, and its pathology? I am talking about the skin in its impact upon the mind, in other words about what I have called the *skin ego*, and not about skin disorders as such, although they often relate to weaknesses in the organization and functioning of the ego. If you will allow me a rather condensed formulation, I would say that in Freud's time the repressed was that part of psychic life that related to sex: that is why he understood what sort of desires hysterics were expressing through their bodily symptoms. Now that the sexual is no longer taboo and with the loosening of morality, the development of contraception, and access by women and the young to sexual freedom, the repressed of today is the body—the sensory and motor body. In the era of the third industrial revolution, the revolution of information, nuclear energy, and the video, the repressed is the body. In our society, in which the language of machines and the mass media has become so predominant, in which long-distance communications have been perfected, generalized, and automated, and in which the production and possession of ever more sophisticated manufactured objects in indefinite numbers are experienced as obligatory, physical and affective closeness is being unlearnt, and the sense of natural realities and ecological balances is being lost. We are forgetting the biological roots of man and of the mind.

But let us stay within my own area of experience. Psychoanalysis has taken a great interest in investigating psychic *contents*—phantasies, anxieties, memory screens, etc.—as means and conditions of access to psychic conflicts and the neurotic symptoms that stem from them. It has enquired very little into the problem of the *container*, which was taken for granted until it encountered cases—narcissistic personalities, borderline states, certain psychoses—in which the psychic container had so manifestly deteriorated or failed that the first reaction was to declare them unanalysable. How is the container formed—or, rather, these containers that are stuck together, or superimposed with an intercalary gap, or substituted for one another? Direct psychoanalytic investigation of children through drawing and play and reconstruction during the treatment of adults of damage suffered by the child's mind allow us to understand how skin-to-skin, body-to-body contact between the young baby and his mother (as well as with people in his close environment) conveys elementary forms of meaning that each sense organ, in proportion to its degree of maturity, can then pick up and develop in its own register. Connections are made between these different registers, always related to what people around him show the child that they have understood of his desires, needs, and anxieties. This twofold network of stimulation that is agreeable and reinforces energy, and of mutual meanings, produce the first version of the ego, the skin ego. The skin ego is a screen that gives protection from excessive excitation and that filters the first communications.

The tactile envelope, which is also an envelope of warmth, softness, and firm holding (but also of cold, roughness, and slackness), articulates with the sonorous envelope (the bath of words, music, and the melody of the mother's voice), with the envelope of tastes and smells, and later with the envelope of colours—I am not trying to give an exhaustive list. The skin ego is at once a sac containing together the pieces of the self, an excitation-screen, a surface on which signs are inscribed, and guardian of the intensity of instincts that it localizes in a bodily source, in this or that sensitive zone of the skin. My research work bears upon two points: on the one hand, studying the various configurations that the skin ego may take—the carapace skin ego, the muscular second skin (already described, respectively, by the English analysts Frances Tustin and Esther Bick), the sieve ego skin and the envelope of suffering (I borrow this expression from Micheline Enriquez), the dream film, the invulnerable and idealized narcissistic envelope (observed in aviators by André Missenard), and so on—and, on the other hand, associating each deficiency in psychic functioning with a particular type of early pathogenic impingement by the environment upon the skin ego as it was being formed and specifying the type of psychoanalytic work that needs to be undertaken when faced with such a deficiency. It is evident, for example, that the interpretative function of the psychoanalyst, which is essential and sufficient in the treatment of neuroses, must be preceded in the treatment of disturbances of the skin ego by the exercise of a containing function, which re-establishes a minimum of continuity in the skin ego, and by the exercise of a pre-symbolic function, which ensures intersensorial connections and contact in the form of mental representations between data belonging to different registers (sensory, motor, rhythmic, postural, mimetic, and emotional). More recently I have improved upon my grid for analysing the skin ego by establishing systematic correspondences between the biological functions of the skin and the psychological functions of the ego. I have thereby revealed nine functions of the skin ego (support, containment, excitation-screen, individuation, and so on), which are laid out in detail in my latest book, *The Skin Ego* (Dunod, 1985; English trans. Yale University Press, 1989).

GT: The new American therapies have taken a lot of interest in the body. In France you have only discovered bio-

energy very recently, together with all those bodily techniques that were devised in the United States more than
twenty years ago now. It is as though France were lagging
behind. 'Rebirth', Janov's primal scream, 'feeling therapy',
and so forth, are sprouting up there like mushrooms: these
therapies are centred upon the experience, analysis, and
treatment of the body (just as one says 'treatment of texts').
What strikes me, as a French Canadian, is that a traditionally Puritan country like the United States, which has a
Protestant majority, should have developed this marked
interest in the body, whereas in a Latin country like France
it has taken much longer. However, the French seemed better prepared by their Latin culture to play with the body. . . .

DA: Latin culture is also a culture of reason. Freud already
remarked that the French were too rationalist to accept
psychoanalysis and the existence of the unconscious easily.

GT: How is it that these bodily therapies emerged instead
in the United States? There, people are being taught how to
touch one another, recover elementary body contact, take
pleasure in it, and be reborn.

DA: It is precisely this that has been repressed in the
industrialized West. There is a great need to re-learn to
touch, to touch the points that awake new sensations, to
touch the points of pleasure and pain, to re-establish well-
being within one's own skin, to massage, envelop, breathe,
and listen with one's body, and to speak to other bodies.
Reflecting upon the ins and outs and outcomes of these
experiences and their excesses or shortcomings is the task of
psychologists and psychoanalysts. But guiding their practice
is another matter, the task of parents with their little
children, kinestherapists, and lovers. In the United States
there is undoubtedly the advantage, and this is not confined
to psychology, of greater freedom of invention in all areas.
Every possible avenue is explored, whereas in the Old World

a new venture must be inscribed within orthodox Marxism, orthodox Freudianism, orthodox Darwinism, or orthodox quantum theory in order to be admitted and considered.

GT: In other words, in France there is ultimately less interest in whether something new actually does or does not work. Instead, it must be logical. . . .

DA: Exactly. I would also say that the Americans, perhaps because they have no ancient roots, and in default of having them, are always looking for something 'new': they are great consumers. New things wear out very quickly among them. Psychoanalysis has interested them since 1910; it invaded the hospitals and universities from 1945 onwards. Now it is losing steam. It is worn out. Psychoanalysts themselves have been swept up in this social trend of repressing the body. The rule of abstinence not only forbids gestures and acts of love with one's patient or burdening oneself physically with him. It has become a rule that means holding one's distance. The analyst protects himself, for example, from any smells, affects, or rhythms that might emanate from the patient. Respiratory difficulties, intestinal rumblings, and muscular contractions are regarded as null and as not having happened. Lacanism has accentuated this tendency: only what passes through and in language should be taken into account. Certainly where infantile experience before the acquisition of speech is concerned, the aim of analysis is to allow the patient to reach a point where he can put words to these sensations, experiences, and anxieties. It may be that bodily techniques have broken through with greater ease in the United States, where the human and social sciences have remained closer to a behaviourist schema. Even if—and rightly so in my opinion—psychoanalysts, whether American or French, criticize the lack of theoretical foundation and methodological rigour that the practitioners and inventors of these new theories display, it still remains the case that their multiplication and popularity is an alarm signal that warns us that here there is material that needs to be taken into account and elaborated! I am tempted to say that either psychoanalysis will survive by renewing itself and integrating everything to which these bodily therapies draw attention, in which case it will survive as it renews itself, or else in the year 2000 it will be shelved in the storehouse of obsolete accessories that are no longer talked about except in courses on the history of medicine and mentalities.

GT: At the present time, in your own practice, how does this preoccupation manifest itself? I think the couch still exists, but do you give the patient the possibility of seeing you? Have you changed the layout of classical analysis?

DA: Analytic work can be done with a patient lying down who does not see us, but also in certain cases with a patient seated facing who does see us. If he prefers to sit on a chair, on the floor, or on the couch—well, let him adopt any spatial position that helps him to communicate what he has to say. Certain patients might exceptionally be able to have an important session over the telephone.

GT: Is that so?! . . .

DA: They have difficulty in having it in our presence because elements of persecutory anxiety then assume excessive proportions with them.

GT: But do you yourself take patients on the telephone, M Anzieu?

DA: I do not offer treatment by telephone. I am not 'S.O.S. Friendship' or 'S.O.S. Help'. But if one of my patients cannot come to his session because he is having a fit of depression or is in the midst of a crisis of persecutory anxiety, and he phones me to excuse himself, I might possibly ask him what was going on and attempt to carry out some interpretative work with him on the spot during the time of his session. I am not saying that I do this at every telephone call, because that would quickly become a means of blackmail on his part.

GT: You have only been doing psychoanalysis in this way for twelve to fifteen years. You have changed your practice. . . .

DA: I have made it more flexible. There has always been a fairly wide diversity among the ways in which analysts work because they themselves are recruited from among different types of psychic functioning. This is not new. The problem is to know whether the analyst is modifying an element of the analytic setting because it suits him, in which case it is an open door to plenty of aberrations, or whether he is doing it in accordance with a theoretical finding, and because this modification makes better contact possible with his patient's unconscious.

GT: One could note that psychoanalysis has itself changed a lot in general and adapted to custom. There was a certain number of rules in the not very distant past, including that of the 'couch', which meant that the patient could not see the analyst, for reasons with which you are familiar (and which are perhaps justified on the theoretical plane: this solitude on the patient's part, facing himself and his phantasies, was deemed necessary). The rule is now changing on this point. As for the rule of abstinence, which implied the obligation to have no physical contact between patient and analyst, this has not been respected by everyone either, in the United States at very least, and certainly in France. Many therapists, at certain moments in the analysis, no longer consider it sensational to go against this rule that was once regarded as fundamental: they find themselves touching their patient, reassuring him physically, putting an arm around his shoulder, and weeping with him under certain circumstances.

Like Julien Bigras in Quebec, to name but one: when his patient touches him, he lets himself be touched. So rules are changing to such a degree that one could ask serious questions about what ultimately remains of the fundamental rules of classical psychoanalysis. The issue you yourself broached a little while ago is the following: if psychoanalysis wants to survive, it must evolve, but might it adapt to the point of questioning its own fundamental rules, to the point of 'perverting' itself?

DA: I have two replies to make. First point: it is not at all the same thing to take a patient lying down and to receive one face to face. The difference, as I was saying in our last interview, is between the liberation of desire on the one hand, and restructuring the ego on the other, which conditions the strength and orientation of desire towards goals and objects. If the patient's ego is sufficiently organized, it is a matter of leading him to slacken his defences so that desire can make itself known: then the lying-down position without seeing the analyst is necessary. But if we are dealing with patients who are suffering from serious flaws in the ego, from deficiencies in certain psychic functions, or whose need to find auxiliary egos in their early environment was not satisfied in childhood, it is preferable, even indispensable, for them to find with their analyst—in addition to verbal dialogue—the visual exchange and communication through mime and posture that they have not made sufficient use of previously.

For the analyst, this is not a question of personal convenience: he diagnoses what is provoking the patient's suffering, inhibitions, and setbacks, and as a result determines how and on what he is going to work.

Second point: the rule of abstinence, and the possible perversion of the analysis if it is not observed. For me, the prohibition on touching remains a prohibition that is not only fundamental for the development of the analytic process in treatment, but also for the development of the psychic apparatus in the child. The oedipal prohibition that comes later on with the discovery of the difference between the sexes and generations, and which forbids incest and its symmetrical complement parricide or fratricide, only takes on its structuring value if there has already been a first prohibition, which is that upon touching. This coincides in time with the acquisition of speech and walking, and it represents one of the conditions for acquiring speech. If in fact the growing child persists in taking his mother's or an adult's hand and leading them up to an object he needs or wants so that that hand can give it to him, then there is no reason to make the effort to ask for it with words, and an environment that is too weak avoids opposing him with prescriptions, arguments, and explanations that might introduce him into the field of dialogue, dialectic, and verbal thought. The prohibition upon touching one's own genital organs and masturbating, which was so vivid in Freud's time, has diminished considerably. Children's sexual games are tolerated. By contrast, children are always forbidden to touch the genital organs of their parents (and, implicitly, of adults). But prohibition goes beyond and precedes the field of sexuality as narrowly defined. As soon as the child is walking, he is forbidden to touch dangerous objects or to touch in a way that gives hurt or destroys. This prohibition on touching seems to me to be structuring. I have given a lot of thought to this, but I have not yet definitively come to conclusions about it. For the moment let us say that the baby's original phantasy in relating to his mother is one of having a common skin with her. In imagination each of them develops in different parts of a single skin, which allows them immediate exchange and contact. The prohibition upon touching detaches the baby and his mother from this over-close contact. This is the moment when the mother picks up the baby less often, when she holds him less closely to her, stops suckling him, or gives him more solid food on a spoon, that is, with her hand. The psychic function of the hand, a function of taking or grasping objects, words, and thoughts, supersedes the containing function vested in the surface of the body. This is a crucial moment. . . .

GT: Of rupture. . . .

DA: Yes, of rupture in the psychic organization and the constitution of the ego. This includes first of all a skin ego and then a hand ego. This distinction seems crucial to me—whence the necessity to take account of it in treatment. If one has to deal with seriously ill patients, full-blown psychotics or autistic children, for example, I do not think that one can use psychoanalysis with them; or, at least, that one can embark upon it without resort in the first instance to techniques like damp wrapping (or a 'pack') or rhythmic rocking, body-to-body contact, and play with water or clay, and so on. Where not even the original skin ego exists, it has to be made. But it does already exist in most of the patients whom we take into analysis. The prohibition upon touching is part of the rule of abstinence, and it must be maintained as a structuring principle for the third dimension, that of space, the acquisition of depth, exit from symbiosis, access to motor and muscular independence, and entry into the semantic field. Psychoanalysis can take place when physical separation between the analyst's body and the patient's body is maintained. But one can permit the psychic, not physical, approach involved in the exchange of looks and postural identification. It is up to the psychoanalyst, in his internal work of elaborating interpretation, to find words that are symbolic equivalents of what was missing in the tactile exchanges between the baby and his mother. He is in fact now dealing not with a young baby, but with an older child, an adolescent, or an adult—in other words, with someone who has passed in body beyond the state of touching, even if psychically he has remained stuck there; with someone, for example, who has reached puberty and the potential for genital sexual fulfilment. It is through transposition onto

the plane of discourse—discourse in which the psychoanalyst's body is also speaking on a pre-linguistic and infra-
verbal level—that active communication is going to be established about the patient's anxieties and phantasies and the
zones of weakness in his ego. Ordinary language actually
puts it well, and our patients express it thus: 'What you said
touched me.' Or again, 'The look or gesture that you made
towards me touched me.' One can in fact touch the psyche
otherwise than by touching the body. And this is what it is to
be an analyst.

On my part, it has on more than one occasion been enough
for me to imagine in silence that I was making a bodily
gesture of comfort towards a patient in distress when verbal
explanation was inadequate for that patient to recover a
minimum of narcissistic security: in no case did it go so far as
a bodily approach. You asked me a little while ago about the
French Canadian psychoanalyst who allows himself sometimes to weep with his patients, to hug them, or to put his
head in the hollow of their shoulder. Let us say that he does
not set limits where I do. I find that that opens the door to
sexual seduction, or interminable mothering, or reciprocal
confession. It seems to me that it is fundamentally important
to uphold this prohibition if one wants to preserve both the
analytic process and the patient's respect for himself.

GT: But Bigras is North American: he is trying something
that is certainly new and unorthodox in psychoanalytic
terms. And this new thing 'works'. At least it worked in the
experience that he described in his book, *Le psychanalyste nu*
[The Naked Psychoanalyst] (Robert Laffont, 1979). The fact
that this patient is in a position today to live with herself and
be socially integrated, something she was incapable of before
her analysis, demonstrates that at least in this case that type
of 'wild' analysis works. . . .

DA: So much the better for this woman, if it helped her. But
a method cannot be validated by a single case. For one

success, how many failures? My experience, and that of my colleagues who have had to take back into classic psychoanalytic treatment certain patients who had previously had an experience of bodily psychotherapy, leads us to conclude the opposite. Sometimes bodily contact did do them some good during the session itself, but its cessation plunged them into stark disarray and confronted them with an impossible weaning, because for these patients the distinction between outside and inside and the sense of continuity of their existence was far from being secure; the paradox of a treatment that in reality only made up for their deficiency in order just as quickly to deprive them of it again carried their depression to its utmost extreme. This is the kind of paradox that can drive people mad! Sometimes, in the case of young women whose male analyst accepted or proposed bodily contact (while avoiding the genital zones), there was a rapid transition from narcissistic reassurance to erotization of the body surface. These patients would leave their sessions in a state of increasingly unbearable diffuse sexual excitement, which invaded and clouded their psychic functioning and blocked the psychoanalytic process. In such a situation what was to become of 'free' association of ideas? Freedom of thought, and even the possibility of thinking, were paralysed.

In one case, bodily contact would promote symbiotic fusion, but in a way that accentuated anxiety about loss of the object; in another case, it aroused a mixture of real persecution and seduction, which, as they were overlaid upon persecutory and seductive phantasies, made the latter all the more active and all the less analysable.

In a collective work directed by my friend René Kaës and in which I participated, *Crise, rupture et dépassement* [Crisis, Rupture, and Beyond] (Dunod, 1979), we concentrated on the case of a psychotherapy and then psychoanalytic treatment that started with a medical act of bodily touching, and examined the difficulties the psychotherapist had in detaching himself from the repetitious effects of this inaugural contact.

Called in by the doctor in charge of the case to the bedside of a prostrate patient, this psychiatrist, who especially practised relaxation, succeeded by putting his hand on her through the bed-covers in getting her to emerge from her mutism and accept the principle of an analytic psychotherapy. The latter began in fits and starts before becoming increasingly regular, and was interrupted by numerous episodes of acting out on the patient's part, who set about undressing and/or snuggling up against her analyst and begging him to touch her over the whole surface of her body so that she could feel that she had one. This colleague needed a lot of tact, firmness, and mastery of his countertransference in order to channel its manifestations without giving in either to anger or seduction, to find adequate interpretations, and to lead the patient very gradually to allow and observe the proper limits of the psychoanalytic situation. One of the decisive interventions that he came up with was as follows: he pretended, using a technique derived from psychodrama, to go over this woman's body as she lay on the couch, but without touching her, his hand remaining twenty centimetres above her, while verbalizing that he was putting her body together, unifying it, and bringing it to life.

But it is good to strike a fair balance among criticisms. I could cite just as many cases of second treatments where the previous analyst had worked honestly and effectively upon oedipal conflicts while remaining inattentive to the existence of deficiencies or excesses in various sensorial or motor stimulations in the patient, in particular in all those that belong to the tactile area. The work of re-analysis has then consisted in mentally reconstructing with the patient the origin and effects of these deficiencies or excesses, but employing only verbal thought (inhibition or damage to which could also be analysed along the way) and speech.

GT: You do not allow yourself to be touched physically, but you do accept being touched emotionally. Many psychoanalysts consider that even that is going too far. Analysis is no longer possible, they would say, because it is fusion, and the analyst no longer represents the blank surface that he is supposed to represent for the patient.

DA: I would turn your objection around and say: if the analyst remains a blank surface, he is going to reproduce for the patient the picture of an indifferent mother, inaccessible, the image of the 'dead' mother described by André Green as being at the root of certain 'blank' psychoses. Now it is precisely from such a maternal image that many of the borderline patients that I have mentioned are suffering. If the analyst—and this is a general rule that I have formulated and to which I stick—and if the analytic session reproduce one of the pathogenic elements in the patient's childhood, the analyst can use all his interpretative virtuosity, but the psychoanalytic situation will do nothing but make the patient even more ill, because it will be repeating, reinforcing, and making inexorable the primitive pathogenic situation. It therefore helps to suspend, at least temporarily, the relevant parameter in the psychoanalyst's instructions and interventions and in the material setting, and to make adjustments to the situation.

GT: But what you say here is new compared with what you were saying only eight or ten years ago, M Anzieu. . . .

DA: I am capable of evolving, you see. . . . Yes, a blank surface, if you insist, but with the reservation that it must not be a pure reproduction of an indifferent mother. The analyst is a reflecting surface, more an echo than a mirror, or, rather, he is a sonorous mirror who echoes at a deep level what is going on in the patient and the way in which the latter's mind is functioning.

GT: Events have been taking place in France for some time that involve a form of psychology that was developed some fifteen years ago in the United States and is in a sense opening its little European branch. I say 'little' because the European movement is relatively new. It is called l'Association Européenne de Psychologie Humaniste [the European Association of Humanist Psychology]. It is within the tradition of Rollo May, the American existentialist who himself claims affinity with Sartre, and who is trying to introduce into psychology concepts borrowed above all from philosophers like Kierkegaard, Husserl, and Sartre, and also from innovators like Rogers and Jack Gibb, who worked with Kurt Lewin who popularized the whole group dynamics movement in 1946. Gibb detached himself gradually from the American Psychological Association in order to found, with several others, this Humanist Association, which distinguishes itself very clearly from the experimental psychologists, since the humanist psychologists have as object what interests you and me: the human being. In the United States, at least, people noticed that the objects of 'scientific' psychology were no longer human beings, but were rats or other animals subjected to various experiments in the laboratory. Human beings, so the humanist psychologists said, were being reduced to the level of animals that were being flayed for experimental purposes. You are familiar with the very vigorous attacks that have been launched upon behaviourists like Skinner or his predecessor Watson, and which have multiplied in the United States during these last decades. The same reaction is developing in France. You are not part of this humanist movement; however, it is also very much interested in the body. We have seen the increasingly prominent place that the body is occupying in your thinking and practice. Could you clarify how you relate to these movements, especially in the use that they make of the body?

DA: I am going to repeat myself: it does not seem to me to be necessary, except in severe and extreme cases of pathology, to resort to actual touching in order to improve a patient's psychic functioning. Experience shows me that it is sufficient to resort to symbolic touching: one can touch with the voice. In ordinary language we say 'make contact with someone' or 'be in good contact with a person'. This demonstrates very well that while the first origin of contact is tactile, contact is transposed metaphorically to other sense organs and other sensory areas. What strikes me as specifically analytic is finding, by relying on various sense organs and various sensory fields, verbal equivalents for the primitive exchanges that introduce the infant to the world of signifiers—exchanges that then need to be abandoned in order for the being to develop. Otherwise, the symbiotic dependence that you were mentioning a little while ago would be a permanent state. I am glad to hear this initiative called 'humanist'. I recognize that academic psychoanalysis tends to close in upon itself and vacate the fields of sensoriality, tonicity, motoricity, and even affectivity. As soon as a field is left free, it is occupied by others. There is room for the whole world under the sun, including oases, deserts, and mirages. My own personal work aims to articulate a practice with a theory, and a theory with a practice. Psychoanalytic theory has proved itself sufficiently to provide us with a solid and relatively open framework within which it is possible to find room to enlarge upon data such as those on which bio-energy or humanist psychology place emphasis. But, and I insist upon this, this enlargement of data must be performed within a framework indissociable from the former—the framework of the psychoanalytic code of practice.

Groups

G T: We will approach the problem of groups. You have written several books on this subject. I am not going to cite all of them, but among others you published in 1968 *La Dynamique des groupes restreints* [The Dynamics of Small Groups], with J.-Y. Martin, a revised and enlarged eighth edition of which was published by the Presses Universitaires de France in 1985. You published with Dunod in collaboration with the other members of your team at C.E.F.F.R.A.P. the two volumes of *Travail psychanalytique dans les groupes* [Psychoanalytic Work in Groups] (1972 and 1982), and then alone, also with Dunod, *Le Groupe et l'inconscient* [The Group and the Unconscious] (1975), a work on the theme of the imaginary in groups which has been translated into English, Spanish, Italian, and Portuguese. You have collaborated in a whole series of collective works that have appeared in Dunod's series *Inconscient et culture* [The Unconscious and Culture] that you co-edit with René Kaës and in which you show your interest in groups.

And of course you have 'practised' for a long time in groups, with a view either to psychotherapy or the participants' personal formation.

One thing seems to me very open to criticism when Americans get into groups: it is the bewildering speed with which instructors in Bethelian formation (which includes Janov's primal scream, 'feeling' therapy, and all the movements that tend to spring up there like mushrooms around masters in thinking like Frederick Pearls, this time with Gestalt therapy) have propagated cells and group communes of that type practically everywhere in the United States. 'Groupitis' was an American phenomenon before it became a French one. What is more serious is that non-psychologists, having taken one or two courses with Janov, claim to be 'primal scream' therapists. Anyone at all can call themselves a group leader or therapist—it is not a protected title. Plenty of quacks have penetrated the market and offer makeshift formation or healing. Everyone can start a group or sell a group in the United States. These are often people interested in immediate material profit. They use an incongruous mixture of techniques, they throw everything together into a sort of melting-pot, without smell, colour, or taste. They do anything at all. This undoubtedly has the result of offering momentary relief to some of the patients who come to them, but the immediate or after-effects could turn out to be dangerous for people who had up to then had good psychological defences and who crack all of a sudden under the impact of a method that is too intensive and too brutal. One has seen cases of decompensation and even of suicide. To crown it all, group leaders such as this call themselves 'humanists'! It is risky to throw oneself wholeheartedly and with impunity into a group. I wonder whether such practices exist in France, and whether the French 'market' is familiar with this phenomenon?

DA: Yes. . . .

GT: ... and how ultimately is the public to be protected?

DA: There you are raising a difficult question, because as
soon as one wants to define a profession legally one is imposing not only usable rules for training and practice, but also
titles, diplomas, controls, selections; and, at least, in France
one is quickly suspected of having corporatist ambitions and
of wanting to reinstate privileges and privileged occupations. What is more, there is a risk that codifying it would
rigidify the profession. State intervention does not seem
desirable, either in the private life of individuals or in
occupations that concern the most intimate aspect of the
personality, its psychic functioning. In a free country, freedom of initiative is ultimately fundamental; freedom for
each to do what he feels he can do, and to be judged by the
results. If it is not working, one is supposed to be aware of it.
The trouble is that this reasoning, which is valid in the
technical domain (if one builds a house that does not stand
up, then obviously everyone notices), is far less secure in
psychological matters, because the elements of appreciation
are more subtle and biassed by influence, seduction, and
illusion. The unconscious phantasies of those involved and
their resistance to seeing themselves and others as they are
can blind them to the shortcomings and defects in the internal construction work that has come their way.
   Let us pass on to a more sociological and almost philosophical level of reflection. It seems to me that the evolution of the
industrialized societies is heading, on the one hand, towards
a small number of highly specialized people who are trained
in an advanced way, have a precise area of competence, and
to whom the State must allow great freedom of life and
thought, and, on the other hand, towards a large number of
professionals who are more superficially trained, polyvalent,
and responsible for sorting out elementary questions and
responding to immediate social need in determinate sectors.
This professional dis-qualification can be observed among

workers in industry, in education, and among intellectuals and reseachers. Why should psychoanalysts, psychologists, and those who form and lead groups be spared by this evolution? Second reflection. The burgeoning of interest in groups and group methods needs to be seen within the context of our highly competitive societies, in which social competition is constantly active. Group experiences offer, by contrast with social storms, a haven of mercy and a place in which the individual can experience a positive shared feeling, and in which he can communicate without a fight and take stock of himself without having to confront himself too starkly. The participants in such groups are not usually people who work together or who have been summoned to work together; since they therefore have no reason to feel in competition with one another, they can disclose their psychic functioning to the others and can reveal themselves in their desires, needs, and anxieties in a way that bears no consequences. In this sense these groups are 'in camera', cut off from social realities, and are in artificial paradises. One might wonder about the massive resort by individuals to this sort of drug habit, to this addiction to groups. Another possible explanation would be that, in a world in which the demographic explosion is leaving less and less room for each individual and in which relationships are becoming ever more economic, bureaucratic, and indifferent, the small group provides the opportunity to rediscover primary human contact among its members.

GT: You are therefore saying that you are helpless and resigned?

DA: I share Freud's serene realism and constructive pessimism about projects that claim to change the basis of human nature or to control social evolution: which is not at all the same thing as you impute to me. I only know one attitude in the face of the inevitable wear and tear to psychological, pedagogic, moral, and political systems, and in the face of their alteration and perversion—what Aristotle called their 'corruption': to maintain by what one says, what one writes, and what one does, the straight grain that others warp; to clarify, explain, and strengthen the theoretical and technical framework that informs practice while at the same time leaving it open to innovation, a framework that also ensures responsibility in its application. This is what orthodoxy means to me. Georges Favez, from whom I have learned a great deal on his couch, in conversation, and from his writings (which I tried to collect into a single volume, *Être Psychanalyste* [To Be a Psychoanalyst], also with Dunod, 1976), distinguished between resistance *to* psychoanalysis (an external resistance that has been returning in strength for some time) and the resistance *of* psychoanalysis: its capacity to resist those who undermine it from within. Formative and fertile rather than wild and destructive psychoanalytic work is possible in groups, provided that there is a setting that allows each participant: first of all, to remain confident of existing (whence the function that is proper to the team of psychoanalysts of containing the sensations, affects, and phantasies that threaten the unity and continuity of each member and of the group); secondly, to feel his own true feelings and articulate them with representations, words, and thoughts (whence the group psychoanalyst's function in assisting symbolization); and, thirdly, to have a differentiated awareness of his own psychic functioning and that of the others (whence the psychoanalytic function of interpretation properly so called). My experience, and that of my fellow team members, has confirmed us in the view that it is necessary to define a specific setting for each type of group (related to its aims and composition); to transform into verbal thought the experience that group members have been invited to live through within this setting; and to analyse fairly regularly among ourselves our imaginary relationship to groups in general, or to this or that group in particular, as well as our emotional and intellectual disagreements. This is what René Kaës has called 'inter-transferential analysis'. I am sorry to say and to find that the less a group leader observes these necessities, the more its participants run risks of psychological destructuring and even physical self-destruction.

GT: M Anzieu, you do not like travelling very much. You seldom leave your own country, unlike the American practice. There are schools that have been built around certain names, something that you do not like very much because you deplore the illusion of having to find a master or a God. ... Nevertheless, this psychoanalytic work that you are doing on groups, which represents a pole that is all the more interesting because it differs palpably from group practice in the United States or elsewhere—this work is completely unknown to the North American public, which is more familiar to me than to you. People do not know enough about what you are doing: they know what is done at Bethel, and they are up with what is being done in California, and at Palo Alto. Does setting up at a school not interest you?

DA: As I have said, I am profoundly reluctant to put myself forward as a master in thinking.

GT: As a model. . . .

DA: That is not the same thing. As a teacher and researcher I inevitably offer a certain model, let us say in intellectual rigour, attention to the other, and clarity in expounding my ideas—an example, any way, rather than a model. But I have never tried to have disciples. When collaborators, or better still, unknown individuals who have only read one of my books or heard one of my papers confirm by their observations or experiences hypotheses that I have made, it is precious to me from the scientific point of view. The fact that I also derive personal, let us even call it narcissistic, satisfaction from it is only natural. But I do not seek it out for its own sake. I have seen too much around me of the errors and intellectual follies into which this could lead those who let themselves fall into the trap of the narcissistic seduction exerted by a so-called master: I have perhaps gone to extremes in guarding myself against occupying that position.

None the less, your criticism of me needs to be tempered. I am not completely unknown. It has been said, and written, that I have originated a French school of group psychoanalysis. My books are not best sellers. But they are read, re-read, commentated, discussed, and used as working tools by my colleagues and fellow workers, and they play a part in the training of psychoanalysts, psychologists, and group leaders. This is enough to put me at peace with my ideal requirements.

GT: For the sake of our readers, could you sum up the work that you do with groups? Could you start by telling us about your experience of psychodrama? What has a man like you found in psychodrama, which was invented by Moreno? You knew Moreno. . . .

DA: I very much liked the man, his sensitivity, creativity, warmth, generosity, and ability to enter quickly into deep contact with another person. I was less enamoured of his theoretical woolliness and his utopia of a universal harmony brought about by generalized psychodrama.

GT: At first sight one could wonder how psychodrama, which is a representation of the psyche on a stage, fitted into your scheme of thought and into your practice. What interested you in it, while transforming it, since with others you have made efforts to render psychodrama psychoanalytic?

DA: In the method which I practice and which I expounded in my first book, *Le Psychodrame analytique chez l'enfant et l'adolescent* [Analytic Psychodrama with Children and Adolescents] (P.U.F., 1958), there is no stage raised above the level of the spectators: the place for play is level ground, and spectators properly so-called are not admitted. All the members of the group cannot of course participate at the same time in all the psychodramas, as that would be chaotic. Each takes turns at being actor and observer, but where adults are concerned, those who have remained observers of a play will afterwards exchange their impressions of it with the actors, in a shared analysis whose aim is to disentangle the meaning of what has happened. Neither is there, as Moreno was, a director of the play who fixes the scenario and gives directions to the actors while remaining outside the scenes. That was a privileged position, almost one of demiurge; what is more, Moreno admitted it himself. Once again, I do not want to be either master or demiurge. A psychodramatist is brought in on occasions to take a role and to interact psychodramatically with the patients or members of a formation group, and by doing so he exposes himself to revealing something of himself to the view of others. He does so in a manner that remains controlled, because he is trying to play in a way that is useful to the patient, to draw him out and disinhibit him, to confront him and oblige him to react, or to enable him to disclose a conflict, a weakness, or a hidden resource. But he can only succeed in this if he is spontaneous in his play, at the risk of introducing into it personal elements to which he then needs to return to his private reflection. A psychodramatist exposes himself more than a psychoanalyst, but this gives him in return a more intense contact with his own unconscious. Psychodrama, from this point of view, as well as other group activities, has for a long time been a need in my own personal psychic economy.

GT: Without wishing to go into overly technical details, there are nonetheless fundamental differences between your practice and that of Moreno. For you, for example, acting out is a regression, whereas for Moreno it isn't at all.

DA: It is not as clear-cut as that. If it is acting out in the psychoanalytic sense of the term—that is, a shift into action that abruptly short-circuits speech and realizes an unconscious desire without the subject noticing—then yes, it is a regression. But acts are also, and before language, signs or indications that are taken by the human environment as messages and which prepare the way for the baby to acquire the linguistic code. The advantage of psychodrama is that it takes place in the zone where verbal language has not yet been disengaged or detached from all pre-verbal and infra-linguistic communication: it unfolds where the two meet. It therefore allows the signifying power of speech to be recharged in bodily experiences. It corresponds to what child psychologists have called the demonstration stage, which is that in which symbolic thought is born. Psychodrama maintains an equal distance from the excess of intellectualism to which the purely verbal methods of psychotherapy or formation expose people, and from that other excess that we have mentioned in connection with humanist psychology and the new bodily methods in groups, in which people tend to content themselves with a non-verbal experience, not taken up either by verbal thought or into an exchange of words. Psychodrama seems to me to be a precise mid-point between bodily expression and verbal communication. There again, practitioners take things more from one side or the other, according to their own personalities. But this openness is one of the strengths of psychodrama.

GT: Which you have used above all with children and adolescents. . . .

DA: For therapeutic purposes. For purposes of formation I have used it with adults. Psychodrama is one of the most effective methods of formation that I know. For a psychoanalytic type of intervention in social organizations whose functioning has been weighed down with internal psychological problems, I have found that representation of their conflicts by the people who are themselves involved is one of the best ways of succeeding in overcoming these conflicts.

GT: There remains the theatrical side of psychodrama, which is found even in analytic psychodrama. For you who love the theatre, I think there is an element here that had to come into play. . . .

DA: There is no doubt about that. I have told you that one of my dreams was to have been an actor. Shall we say that I have sublimated or displaced this longing into the practice of psychodrama. It is obvious that in order to succeed in a psychodramatic activity, one must be stimulated by being seen by others, and get from it voyeuristic and exhibitionistic satisfactions. There are analysts who object to this, and I cast no stones at them: each to his own temperament, and it is for each to find the route through which he communicates best with the unconscious of others.

GT: From psychodrama groups your experience widened to purely verbal formation groups.

DA: In 1956, within the framework of the Marshall Plan for economic aid to Western Europe, some American experts in human relations and group dynamics conducted in Paris the first seminars organized by l'Agence Européenne pour la Productivité. I had the good fortune to be told about this and to have been accepted as a participant. The T-group, a term that I and my fellow team members in C.E.F.F.R.A.P. translated first as 'diagnostic group' and now as 'verbal expression group', was a revelation to me. I had the impression of living through in a fortnight a gripping résumé of my four years of psychoanalysis with Lacan, enlarged by various internal experiences that had not been able to find a place there. I verified the truth of Freud's view, according to which there is only one and the same unconscious at work, whether in the individual intimacy of treatment or in a plural situation: individual psychology is also a social psychology, and there is nothing in social psychology that does not already exist in individual psychology. The intuitions I displayed, the psychoanalytic terms of reference to which I explicitly appealed, and the problems that I set myself or even set the Franco–American pair of monitors (Claude Faucheux and Harold Leavitt) resulted in my being involved successively as observer, as assistant monitor, and as principal monitor in later seminars. In 1962, with half a dozen colleagues who had collaborated with me in analytic psychodrama and/or diagnostic groups (Angélo Béjarano, Jacques-Yves Martin, André Missenard, J.-B. Pontalis, Geneviève Testemale-Monod, and Paulette Dubuisson), I decided to found C.E.F.F.R.A.P.

GT: What do these initials stand for?

DA: The Cercle d'Études françaises pour la Formation et la Recherche Active en Psychologie. We wanted to take up a position at the crossroads between social psychology and psychoanalysis. We held our own seminars. We extended the methods of the T-group and psychodrama from small groups to large groups. But for years we beat our brains to find a theory that would take sufficient account of the findings that went on piling up. We tried several keys—Lewinian, Lacanian, Sartrian—without great success. Freud's famous essay *Group Psychology and the Analysis of the Ego* enabled us to talk about group phenomena rather than to interpret them. The importance of mutual identifications, the quasi-hypnotic fascination that resulted from the massive presence of several individual unconscious minds, and the ambivalence of members towards their leader or monitor did not escape us, but they did not provide a sufficient foundation for a group-psychoanalytic method. It is Melanie Klein who got us out of our difficulty. From other directions we were discovering her work, which was beginning to be translated into French. We heard her ideas being talked about by our child psychoanalyst colleagues, some of whom happened to be wives or companions of one or other of us.

During one of our team meetings, a connection was proposed between what Klein called the paranoid and depressive positions, and the types of anxiety that we were noticing in the formation groups and which we were even feeling on our own account in those situations. This was enlightenment. This idea struck a chord in several of us, and we brought different facets of it into play. Those to whom it meant nothing sooner or later ended up withdrawing from our team. From then on our reflection was conducted with Kleinian concepts.

GT: Could you explain briefly what Melanie Klein meant by these positions?

DA: The paranoid (or persecutory) position makes us dread being invaded not only in our bodies but above all in our minds by a being who is all-powerful, tyrannical, and threatening, who surrounds us, is more an undifferentiated piece of body and mind than a true person, and from whom no frontier or barrier separates and protects us. Here anxiety takes forms of this sort: my body is being penetrated to arouse certain sensations in me, my thoughts are being stolen, or I am being influenced in my desires and ideas—whence my suspicion of all those who display curiosity, interest, or affection towards me. Whence the alternatives: either to attack this persecutor violently if one succeeds in identifying him, or else to withdraw into indifference and insensibility and to take up residence thousands of light years away from him behind an impassable no man's land (which then corresponds to a schizoid position).

GT: And in groups?

DA: Persecutory anxiety shows up in the following manner. You come in full of good will, and you introduce yourself as a psycho-sociologist or as a psychoanalyst who wants to understand the group, or even to help it to function better; it is in fact generally for this reason that you have been called in. Whereas at the opening of play you are hated, distorted, criticized, suspected of the worst intentions, and attacked verbally (I even remember, during an introductory pedagogic seminar for officers who had been selected as instructors at a large military school, that Jacques Ardoino and I were openly threatened with being shot: this was, admittedly, during the Algerian war). Or else, when you have come to see what is going on in the group and on the basis of that to counsel it, give it direction, or diagnose its problems, the group freezes in the schizoid position, nothing happens, and you feel you are being kept at a distance, driven off into another galaxy. It is very different when the group reacts with depressive anxiety. You are taken for somebody very good, for a complete, sensitive, and devoted human person. The group is ashamed in front of you for its weaknesses and its misdemeanours. It declares itself at fault for whatever is wrong, it blames itself, it tells you you can do nothing for it because it has destroyed it own resources, which you cannot give back to it, and at the same time it renders you helpless.

GT: What can a psychoanalyst do in such situations?

DA: He contains the collective emotion, he lets it enter him without being overwhelmed by it, and he does not react as the group expects and prompts him to, either by altercation or by backing off, nor by blame or exhortation. Little by little, he talks about what the participants and he himself are feeling, he puts forward descriptions in which each can recognize himself; and, finally, he may be able to interpret what it is about. If he succeeds, the group abandons its persecutory, schizoid, or depressive 'position' and gets down to work.

The effectiveness of this approach, on which we worked together in the course of a week's residential seminars organized by C.E.F.F.R.A.P., encouraged us to pursue our method and reflections in that direction.

For some years our team was caught up in a shared phantasy or, if you prefer, imaginative belief, that I would today describe as follows, with all the risk of distortion that that involves. We were a joyful bunch of wide-awake babies, firmly clutched to the generous body of a mother who was vast enough for each to find their own place, and where each was mapping out an anatomical or geographical region. Or an even more daring group, which, amidst fear and trembling that were thinly disguised under an apparent hypomanic exultation, was adventuring forth to explore symbolically no longer only the surface but the interior of the maternal body projected into the group object. We were able to remain a cohesive group because this phantasy enabled us to deny any possible rivalry among ourselves. We could become a creative group because our quasi-mythical conquest of the objects contained within the immense belly of this imaginary mother aimed not to destroy them in an explosion of envious and impotent rage, but to appropriate for ourselves the very fecundity of its womb. It is easy for us today to see in our attitude then a successful collective defence against the primitive phantasy that Melanie Klein brought to light and which is one of the characteristic forms of projective identification: the infant's phantasy of getting in imagination into the mother's breast in order to attack in it everything that this breast produces and contains solely for his own pleasure—faeces, unborn babies, and the father's penis—and to cause it all to explode, contents and container alike.

What is denied inevitably comes back. Alongside fertile and happy moments, our team meetings and seminars experienced tensions, crises, and ruptures. I was able to develop what I think is the fundamental notion of 'phantasies of breakup' as being the specifically group version of the hateful envy conceptualized by Melanie Klein and amalgamated with the anxieties of castration and object loss already described by Freud.

GT: You consider that that is your most important contribution to group psychoanalysis?

DA: Not exactly. Although it came first chronologically,
the discovery of phantasies of breakup comes epis-
temologically after that of the 'group illusion'. A collection or
gathering of juxtaposed individuals, more or less aggluti-
nated or cut off one from another, becomes a group when they
are gripped by the following collective imaginative belief:
the group exists, as a reality that is both immanent and
transcends each of them, like a good, exacting, and giving
mother who only has good children, and like an enclosed
room whose walls are lined with mirrors that send on to
infinity the idealized narcissistic reflections of each participant. This is an illusion, but here my thinking has been the
object of plenty of misunderstandings, because this term has
been understood as derogatory, as pejorative, whereas we are
talking about a necessary illusion, which sets up a group
object that is at once internal and external to each member,
with a strong libidinal cathexis, and therefore full of energy,
creating what Durkheim called a collective consciousness.
The group illusion corresponds to the founding moment in
which the group forms itself as such. The following stage
tests out the group's capacity to face up to disillusionment, to
acknowledge structuring boundaries, and to accept and use
the differences among its members.

GT: This use of the term illusion is not Kleinian. You owe it
to Winnicott.

DA: Certainly to Winnicott. But to Freud first of all, who
defined art, religion, and philosophy as illusions, and who
described, without giving it a specific name, the illusion at
community or society level upon which the great forms of
social organization are based—the church and the army, but
also the family, school, and right down to stars' fan clubs: the

illusion that the master or chief or father or hero or God himself loves his subordinates, children, faithful, or fans with an equal love.

To return to Melanie Klein, we find that she never studied groups. But while her women students pursued her work in the directions that she had opened up (direct observation of infants, intensive psychoanalytic work with children, and analysis of the child through the adult in treatment), several of her male disciples—Bion, Ezriel, and Elliott Jaques— were interested in group psychoanalysis and in psychoanalytic intervention in institutions. It must be said that her description of the individual psychic apparatus—a self containing somehow or other an innate ego, an acquired superego, and disparate internal objects that are more or less accepted or rejected by the ego and variously cathected by the drives—is still at present the best available model both for thinking about groups and the phenomena that unfold in them, and for building up an effective method.

In France, within the atmosphere of change in C.E.F.F.R.A.P., J.-B. Pontalis was the first to describe the small group as an 'object' in the Kleinian sense. The late Angélo Béjarano analysed the process of splitting of the transference, the positive transference having rather the tendency to concentrate itself upon the small group and the negative transference to be projected into the large group or the out-group. André Missenard unpacked the play of projective and introjective, imaginary, narcissistic-mirroring, and symbolic identifications among the members of a group. René Kaës specified how a 'group psychic apparatus' is constructed upon the basis of individual psychic apparatuses. His intuition of a 'family psychic apparatus' was taken up and developed by Ruffiot, Eiguer, and Caillot and Decherf, who from that starting point built up a psychoanalytic theory and method for family therapy and therapy with couples.

GT: And you?

DA: I would add three personal contributions to those that
I have mentioned so far. The group object is often split into
two pieces of unequal importance: one is idealized, while the
other is persecuted; and this explains why the phenomena of
the cult of a personality, idea, or idol are inseparable from
the exercise of terror. The group object is primitively a part
object, and I have been able to describe several group constel-
lations according to the type of collective relationship that is
established with such an imaginary object: phantasies of the
breast-group, the mouth-group, the toilet-group, the phal-
lus-group, the persecutor–seducer-group, and the paradoxical narcissistic group. Finally, there is no group without a
common skin, a containing envelope, which makes it possible for its members to experience the existence of a group
self.

Regimes pass away,
but the unconscious remains

G T: Let us now talk about the connections between psychoanalysis and politics. Certain psychoanalysts maintain that it is incompatible for a psychoanalyst who works in the calm and privacy of his consulting room, with its rules whose importance you have reminded us of (and which, even if they are being softened, nonetheless remain the fundamental rules that every self-respecting psychoanalyst must observe)—that it is therefore incompatible for him to take an active and public interest in anything other than his work. How can a psychoanalyst be a citizen? Can he be a militant citizen, belong to a party, attend political meetings, or on occasion demonstrate his opinions in the

---

Readers should be reminded that these interviews took place in 1985.

street? This problem has been raised by several people in your own line of business whom I have met—including Luce Irigaray, so as to hide nothing from you—who gets up, with the tone of voice that you know, and with the passion that she puts into it, to try to demystify this sacrosanct, set-apart, non-engaged role that the psychoanalyst has always reserved for himself.

DA: Here is my personal position. To be a psychoanalyst means giving one's entire listening attention to beings who are suffering; it means accepting the patient with his symptoms, with all his problems, and with something that is still more difficult to admit: with his own mode of mental functioning—for it is always difficult to tolerate and understand another mode of mental functioning, when it is very different from one's own. It also means accepting him with his ideas, beliefs, ideals, and value system, in the uncertainty that I find that I have in knowing whether perhaps he will change them, or whether he will keep them, and this perhaps contrary to ideas that he might have about it himself, and contrary perhaps to my own personal opinion about these ideas and beliefs, or contrary to my prognosis of his possible evolution. I have had in analysis members of the Communist party, revolutionary anarchists, and Maoist sympathizers; I have treated liberal patients, conservatives, and partisans of the extreme Right. I have followed Catholics, Jews, Muslims, and atheists. I analyse their psychic conflicts. I never interpret anything that directly touches their political, religious, or philosophical opinions. It seems a fortunate thing to me, at a time when political régimes, whether of the Right or the Left, are tending to control the opinions of individuals, that psychoanalysis preserves a zone in which thought remains free. Too bad if I seem old-fashioned. What is more, I have seen too much during my life of friends, colleagues, and patients discovering that they had been duped by their political engagements not to feel encouraged in my apoliticism.

GT: But the problem, M Anzieu, is you as citizen. You are a psychoanalyst, of course, but you are also a citizen. Do you see yourself going to demonstrate in the street to challenge a law that you do not accept and which offends your conscience? Could you see yourself, for example, going regularly on television for people to ask you questions about political matters? In other words: the public man that you could also be, and the citizen that you necessarily are, cannot make a show of themselves with impunity when one is a psychoanalyst.

DA: Absolutely. If I want to be a psychoanalyst, remain available to my patients, and provide them with an image of myself that is sufficiently neutral for them to be able to project their phantasies into it, there is no doubt about the accuracy of your analysis.

GT: We return to the necessity for the blank surface.

DA: A surface is needed, but not completely blank. I cannot remain a complete unknown for them, or else they would have no reason to engage with me. They must find, in what they have heard about me, in what they have read, in what they see of my flat, my consulting room, my dress, my physiognomy, and in what they unconsciously sense of my personal history and the conflicts I may have had and whose traces I still bear in my body, and in my manner of being, speaking, and responding—they must find concrete points onto which to hook their transference to me. But if I am already a landscape that is too precise, too marked, there is no longer enough room for the deployment of their unconscious. I must therefore be discreet about my personal choices, which I have made as a citizen and as a man in matters of political problems, social life, and questions of morality. Sharing one's ideas with another is already seeking to influence him.

GT: As you know, psychoanalysts and psychologists have often been reproached in a general way for their conservatism on the political level. It is said that in the end psychology is a depoliticized science dedicated to order, and to the established order. For example, in certain eastern countries one has seen the repressive use to which certain scientific discoveries in psychology have been put.

DA: Nearly all the totalitarian countries—whether of the Left or the Right—prohibit psychoanalysis. Perhaps not psychology: in fact, there can be psychological action, a conditioning of individuals and the masses that is useful to the powers that be in those countries. But I have seen them proscribe knowledge of the individual unconscious, starting with Nazi Germany and Stalinist Russia. The psychologist, like the ethnologist, the anthropologist, and the sociologist, is someone who reflects about man and society with a critical eye. And, in France at any rate, I know at least as many who are reformists or revolutionaries in what they propose as conservatives. We have yet to discover what they are in action. The human and social sciences are regarded as contentious disciplines or ones that risk producing contentious people; they are viewed with disquiet by those in positions of power, whether they are positions of power in the Catholic church or the Communist party. In France, De Gaulle and the Communists were agreed at least on one point: they were against psychoanalysis. A society that respects human liberty is one in which the State, among other things, permits psychoanalytic knowledge and practice. I will now reply to your second question, about street demonstrations. Taking to the street to put pressure that verges on violence, to proclaim by example my disagreement with some decision or other, is something I could only envisage doing if the decision in question involved an extremely serious infringement of liberty, justice, or my country's independence.

As an analyst, I consider that my leading concern is to preserve analysis, that is, a place where one can speak freely without being judged or bullied. As an analyst, I also help people who are facing the violence of psychic drives—love, hate, and self-destruction. I do not respond to this violence that torments them, drives them mad, makes them suffer, or makes their entourage suffer, with counterviolence. I draw their anxieties and desires out into words. By talking to them, I allow them to unravel the web of conflicts in which they have become enmeshed: I lead them to make use of their internal speech—the foundation of all internal freedom—in order to decide either to fulfil their desires, or to defer them, or to renounce them. I would find it difficult to hold a different attitude in life from the one that I hold in analysis. I stand for speaking the truth. I believe in the supremacy of speech over violence in order to resolve problems. Of course, if I am attacked, I defend myself; and if someone wants to make a slave of me, I resist; and until my mouth is gagged, I shall speak and attempt to speak truthfully.

So, you see, in my view a psychoanalytic attitude and a political attitude are incompatible, because political activity requires violence, ruses, opportunism, Machiavellianism, and, in short, behaviour according to strategies—all things that are antithetical to a psychoanalyst's state of mind and vocation and to the possible success of his treatment. We are told again and again in speeches more or less laced with threats about the necessity to engage ourselves politically, and the priority that has to be given to economic and social problems. These problems exist, and they require discussions, struggles, and solutions. But I myself cannot conceive of according them an absolute priority, which would soon risk being transformed into a totalitarian requirement. Man cannot live on bread alone, nor on circuses. Individual happiness, contact with the deep unconscious sources of one's being, affirmation of one's personal singularity, the experience of friendship or love—all this is lived out on the margins of politics, and on the margins of economic and social life. The psychoanalyst is among those who make themselves guardians of these values against all the impingements of party, church, or State. In Hungary the pre-war Fascist régime persecuted psychoanalysts; when Communism came into power, it was the same thing. This did not stop the few Hungarian psychoanalysts from continuing to exercise their profession against wind and tide, even though they had to receive patients in their homes in the evening, for free, and be careful only to take on people who would not denounce them. It is this that has permitted continuity and transmission of psychoanalysis in that country, down to the present day. If the situation in France were to become very disturbing for civil liberties, I would choose to be an engaged citizen. So far, we have been preserved from the various forms of totalitarianism. But I would cease to be an analyst at that moment.

GT: Yes. You cannot be both.

DA: No, I could not go on being both of them. I would, however, like to add a confession. At the age that I have now reached, after the disillusionments my generation has experienced, and after the disappointments that have knocked one down from the height of one's beliefs, I feel jaded, and I no longer believe in the utopias that once exalted and also blinded us, and in whose name many errors, if not actually crimes, were committed. As one of my patients supposed of me on a day on which France was changing government: for me, régimes pass away, but the unconscious remains.

GT: Nowadays one cannot sidestep feminism either, even though it is no longer such a loaded word with the passage of time. The question I would like to put to you is the following: Freud has been the Turk's head of all the American feminists; in France, it began with Simone de Beauvoir, who, in *The Second Sex*, questioned a certain number of sexist preconceptions in the father of psychoanalysis. Freud the spiteful, Freud and his penis, Freud and his pansexualism, Freud and castration—women have had enough of it. In all this there are primal emotive reactions, but also others that are more considered because based upon solid and close reading of Freud. Many women have put their finger upon the Freudian deficiency in matters of understanding the feminine universe, and of what Illich would call conviviality with women. It has been said that Freud understood nothing of feminine psychology, nor of women in general. You who have read Freud closely, do you not feel ill at ease, not in the face of these accusations, but with the movements that are springing up all over the world and which are finally questioning 'male politics'?

DA: The psychoanalytic movement can pride itself on the fact that from the very beginning it has never exercised any discrimination between male and female psychoanalysts. This was an avant-garde position at a time when women were only just beginning to have access to higher education, and not yet everywhere at that. They did not yet have the right to vote, nor access to the major bodies of the State, nor to a whole series of professions. The analyst's calling was open from the start to both men and women who had a talent for and interest in the unconscious, without consideration of sex, confessional membership, ethnic origin, and so forth.

GT: It is in fact one of the rare professions in which we see so many women having had such importance on account of their discoveries.

DA: Indeed—which are the two great names that one could mention after that of Sigmund Freud? Anna Freud and Melanie Klein. Both were women. One could name plenty of others in every country where psychoanalysis is practised.

GT: All the same, the question is more fundamental. Is something amiss at the basis of the Freudian scheme, in his very conception of sexuality?

DA: It seems to me absolutely natural that Freud should not have found everything. He made a considerable number of discoveries, but there is scope for rectifying, completing, improving, and nuancing his contributions. I find myself faced with two contradictory arguments threading their way through the interviews we are having. Sometimes I am told: everything is in Freud (provided he is read in the German text), as though there had been nothing else besides him; and sometimes I get the objection: Freud understood nothing about groups, or Freud understood nothing about femininity.

GT: It is not I making these objections; I am reminding you of them.

DA: Freud carried out an immense and pioneering work. He did not break all the new ground, and he remained dependent upon some of the preconceptions of his time, culture, and personality. Are we any different today? Freud certainly tends to be taken as a Turk's head, as you suggest. Sometimes people are surprised that he had been in love, sometimes they sneer at him for remaining monogamous. They miss no opportunity for reproaching him, because they cannot tolerate the fact that he made such a colossal discovery as that of the unconscious. Let us now go closer to the heart of the problem. It is clear that there is a feminine psychology that is distinct from masculine psychology as Freud envisaged it. Children of both sexes—we are sure of this now—have an intuitive knowledge of the vagina and not only of the penis. Little girls sense it in their bodies. They sense it as a folded sheet and not as a hole. Little boys also have an unconscious intuition of it, which may perhaps be based upon an ancestral experience that has become hereditary. Its cause is of little importance, and remains hypothetical. Children's drawings, children's phantasies, and children's play confirm the fact.

GT: This clearly clashes with Freud. . . .

DA: Yes, but the point on which one meets up again with Freud is this: the vagina can be just as much an object of curiosity and horror for boys as the masculine organ can be an object of desire and fear for women. It is a fact, a fact in phantasy; and it is perhaps a distressing fact that does not help relationships between the two sexes, but that is how it is.

GT: Women say: we have a clitoris and not only labia and an orifice.

DA: Freud spoke of that. He found—and this is a frequent but not universal state of affairs—that little girls' first discovery of sexual pleasure was through the clitoris, and that subsequently (and this is only true for some of them) this pleasure is transferred to the vagina. But I do not think that this is the essential question nowadays. The avenues that lead to pleasure are varied, in men as much as in women, and Western society now permits diversity in these avenues for both sexes. It remains for each man and woman to come to an understanding on this point with the appropriate partner. I think that the fundamental question that arises in an acute way nowadays, with the development of methods of contraception, with the fact that girls and women have acquired great sexual freedom and are no longer handicapped by the threat of unwanted pregnancy, and with the growing equality that they are achieving in the social, professional, and conjugal domains, and as lovers—the important question then becomes the following: there is a fundamental biological difference between males and females in so far as, in mammals, it is the female who bears inside her and gives birth to young, and who has in the first days, weeks, and months of life a decisive influence upon the psycho-biological development of the young. I understand completely that women are trying to escape from a position of inferiority in which they have been kept for too long on the intellectual, social, and political levels. I feel I am with them in their

claims. But analytic experience shows us that the psychological fate of a personality is sealed very early: a bodily and
psychic relationship with a mother and an environment that
are well enough adapted to his needs is an essential element
in the baby's future development; which, so far as the mother
is concerned, presupposes that she devotes herself to her
baby during the first months, and that she suspends her
social, professional, and intellectual appetites until she can
resume them at an opportune moment. The danger that
people will no longer want to look after babies seems to me as
grave a danger for humanity as the demographic explosion.

GT: We are witnessing today a reversal of roles. More and
more men are looking after babies at home: I am not only
thinking of the fact of bottle feeding them, changing nappies,
and physically touching babies. They are taking charge of
them while the mothers go to work. This is happening
increasingly. And in the years to come it seems that this is
bound to be a model that will spread pretty well everywhere
in the industrialized societies.

DA: I agree about the evolution of social roles. Sociology,
ethnology, and anthropology show us that there is the greatest possible diversity in the differentiation of masculine and
feminine, paternal and maternal roles: mankind has truly
tried everything in its history and geography. There is
nothing surprising in that. It does not bother me to see an
evolution taking place in our principles and customs on this
point. Having said that, when you say that this evolution is
inevitable, I am not sure of that, because once one has
assessed the consequences of a state of affairs in the medium
term, one ends up correcting errors and inventing new solutions. Otherwise a whole society is in danger of disappearing.
Certain methods of raising children could be as dangerous
for mankind as the atomic bomb.

GT: All the same, there is a serious problem. A baby born to a couple nowadays is no longer automatically given his father's name: the whole problem of filiation is raised at the same time. Nowadays a child may very well have himself called by his mother's name, and she increasingly keeps her maiden name when she marries. The famous hyphen between her maiden name and her married name is also tending to disappear. She no longer has both names. She has her own. The husband keeps his own, and the child chooses. M Anzieu, how many generations will it take for this child to become neurotic?

DA: In any case it takes three generations to make a neurotic: parents' unconscious relationship with their own parents is repeated or reversed with their children.

Women's right to their juridical, economic, social, cultural, and even onomastic identity has been won in the West and will be passed on from generation to generation—barring something like new Islamic invasions. As for the more or less loudly proclaimed negation of the anatomical, physiological, and psychological differences between the sexes, it will do nothing to change reality, but nothing will be able to change it either, given the profound unconscious roots of such a denial.

GT: Let us return for a moment to being in love. How is it that it is regarded as a regression in psychoanalysis?

DA: It is more subtle than that. Psychoanalysis regards being in love both as a state and as a process. It engages two individuals with one another at extremely different psychic levels. Love between two persons is not solid if it is confined to one level only. Enduring love attaches the two partners at the quadruple level of their neurotic phantasies, their narcissistic ideals, their need for support, and their psychotic nuclei. Their ties may be complementary at the neurotic level, symmetrical at the narcissistic level, reciprocal at the supportive level, and antagonistic at the level of psychotic nuclei, but all this largely escapes those involved. That is why the situation of the lasting couple who undertake to last is a situation that is at once passionate, difficult, and, when all is taken into account, instructive about itself and about the nature of human ties.

Creating a work

G T: You have written literary texts. You have told us that you have published *Contes à Rebours*, which is now out of print.

DA: I am preparing a new edition of it, enlarged by two headings, 'Imaginary Women' and 'Imaginary Societies'. I have not yet found a publisher. I must in fact change.

GT: At twenty years of age you published a collection of poems you had written. . . .

DA: Entitled *Verger*, dedicated to the woman who was to be my wife, and illustrated with drawings by my future brother-in-law. Outside the three of us, this book had not the least success.

GT: You have embarked upon fiction, as you mentioned at the beginning of our interviews. You dream of getting started on a career as a writer, one that you have never had the leisure to carry through. Can you talk to us about this vocation? And these stories?

DA: First of all, I must disappoint you: I am not going to devote myself to that vocation. If I talk about it, it is with irony towards myself. I regard my future as a writer as being behind me. My ambition is confined to completing what I have already done, to sorting out and polishing a few texts that are languishing in my drawers: at least, that is my avowed ambition. But until I reach death's door I shall doubtless entertain the secret ambition of producing a new work. Like Paracelsus, in the story that Borges devoted to him.

GT: Which story?

DA: 'The Rose of Paracelsus.' The great Mediaeval alchemist and metaphysician was being badgered by his favourite disciple: 'Master, people say that you have acquired a marvellous power, that you know how to grow a rose that remains intact when it is put on the fire. Master, tell me whether this is true.' Paracelsus refused to reply. The disciple insisted: 'Master, you are old. Before you die, show me this wonder once.' Paracelsus hesitated, took the rose, threw it in the fireplace, and it was reduced to ashes. The disciple wept: What a lesson! What a disillusionment! When he had left, Paracelsus bent down over the hearth and picked up the rose, intact. I hope to preserve as long as possible, on the internal screen of my thought, this representation of an invulnerable, imperishable part of myself. At whatever age one loses this rose, nothing remains, I fear, but to die.

GT: In fact it is Borges that you would have wished to be.

DA: While writing my stories, and then working on a psychoanalytic study of the psychic work of creativity entitled *Le Corps de l'oeuvre* [The Body of the Work] (Gallimard,

1981), I proved to myself that if I did possess half the qualities necessary to become a novelist, I lacked the other half. This first half was enough to enable me to write stories, essays, and poems; and I tell myself that in a few years' time, when I feel I have really aged, it will be enough, should I so wish, to narrate my memoirs. How can one define it? As the intuition of a directing scheme that one develops to the point of exhausting its logical dynamism. And also perseverance and painstaking care with composition. What I came up against, by contrast, something that does not function in me in a prolonged way, is identification with imaginary figures that would be all mine while not being me, and who would detach themselves from me so as to live their own life outside me and impose it upon me. What Alain de Mijilla, in his book that came out at the same time as mine, beautifully described as *Les Visiteurs du moi* [Visitors to the Ego].

GT: You have been very interested in Robbe-Grillet and Borges, whom you were talking about just now.

DA: These are the two authors who have influenced me most in the writing of my literary texts. Now it is striking that in both these authors the element of the author's identification with his characters remains weak. For them, the essential thing is to start off from an original situation, which they try to develop in a logical fashion in all its consequences or in all its variations. A logic that appears illogical because they stick only to certain elements in the situation. It is a kind of game to which one could undoubtedly apply a mathematical formulation. They construct a whole that corresponds in part to reality, but which, given the characteristics of the elements that make up this whole, is going to produce a certain concatenation or release of consequences that are at once terrifying, picturesque, derisory, tragic, and fantastic. It is the procedure that Cocteau called the infernal machine. The logic of the infernal machine marries up with the symbolic or heroic illusion in the traditional novel because the latter provides the reader with the illusion that the characters are more alive than real life. With the *nouveau roman*, the structure of the story is preserved and systematized; the hero disappears. One of the functions of the narrative even becomes that of showing the 'effacement', the crumbling and disintegration of the one or more characters who would like to pass off as the hero or heroes of the story. The titles that Robbe-Grillet gave his two first novels, *Un Régicide* and *Les Gommes*, illustrate this well.

GT: You were saying that you read Proust's *Á la Recherche du temps perdu* when you were quite young. You speak of Balzac and Flaubert. . . .

DA: I am unable to re-read Balzac and to a lesser degree Flaubert. I get on better with Greek and Latin fiction. With Daphnis and Chloe, for example, in which one sees the romantic genre taking shape, and I still get on with *La Princesse de Clèves*. I prefer Proust, Joyce, and Kafka. . . . The great nineteenth-century novels, whether French, English, or Russian, bore me. When I read current novels that put the same romantic scheme as that of the nineteenth century into modern dress, I have the greatest difficulty in getting into them.

GT: Could you explain your last book but one, *Le Corps de l'oeuvre*? I believe it is a work that is both psychoanalytic and aesthetic.

DA: In that book, I adopted the distinction between the *poïetic*, that is, the study of creativity, the relationship between the author and the work, and the *aesthetic*, which concerns the relationship between the work and the public: which qualities make it arouse interest and pleasure in the user? My work is more a labour of psychoanalytic poïetics than of psychoanalytic aesthetics, but I agree that this separation is often difficult to maintain. If, as I hope, I have enough time and mental vigour, I shall return to the question of art and literature in order to develop a psychoanalytic aesthetic properly so called. What I have tried to say about psychoanalytic poïetics—or, to use a less complicated expression, about the pathways of creativity—is that this pathway comprises five stages. These five stages are not necessarily passed through completely. Neither are they necessarily passed through in the canonical order in which my book presents them. The author might pass successively through the first, the second, and the third stage, then return to the first, jump to the fifth, and then settle down or lose himself in the fourth, moving to and fro.

GT: A seesaw. . . .

DA: No, I see it more as a zigzag or spiral. In any case, these five phases, whatever practical use the creative artist makes of them, seem very distinct to me, because they bring into play different levels of functioning of the personality and psychic qualities, each of which needs to have had a different training. This explains why successful creativity is so rare. Many people have the necessary dispositions to try out the first stage and/or the third or the fifth. It remains that in order to create a real work of art, one that will be recognized as such by a public, it will be necessary to pass at one moment or other, or rather at the opportune moment, through each of these phases. This requires a diversity and flexibility of mental functioning that are not very widespread and are rather exceptional. Would you like me to remind you of these five phases?

GT: Gladly.

DA: The first is traditionally described as inspiration. Psychoanalysts have regarded it rather as a moment of regression. I prefer to take up an expression that Michel de M'Uzan has introduced in France: it is a stage of being seized internally. In the evening or in winter, if one exposes oneself too brusquely or too long without moving, one is seized by, or catches, cold. One never talks of catching heat. The metaphors for creativity used by artists and poets converge. They speak of glacial moonlight, of walking in deep snow, of a mortal sensation of shivering, and of numbness. This contradicts popular imagery, which wants creativity to be fiery. Internal warmth returns later: it accompanies transition to the second and third phases. If it is present prematurely, it gives rise to false creations; the deep creations, those that touch their public deeply, come from the cold. In any case, that is the first stage. In this state of seizure, in fact, one lets go of one's self, one's habitual feelings and thoughts, and one's conscious internal fantasy; one does not know whether this state that one has been seized by belongs to oneself or to someone else, and one does not yet know what the state is. There again, popular imagery, of religious or mystical origin, speaks of going to the most intimate point of self, whereas on the contrary it involves going to the edge, to the frontiers of one's self.

> Close to a heart, at the sources of the poem,
> Between the void and the pure event. . . .

as Valéry wrote.

GT: It is an intuitive experience. . . .

DA: Intuitive, if you like, but also disruptive, giving rise to a split in the personality. One departs from what one considered as the centre of one's self and sets it aside, and one goes to seek a new centre on the periphery, at the extreme of one's self; one adventures to the margins that are also frontiers, and this introduces an imbalance into internal functioning that can be creative as well as decompensating. That is why genius is so close to madness—because I think one can say that an experience such as this corresponds to a brief psychotic moment.

The second phase consists in bringing back to conscious awareness what this regression has made us experience; it means seizing what had seized us, passing from a passive attitude to an active position, no longer abandoning oneself to one's skin but using one's hand. This intuition has a variable content. Sometimes it is an image, sometimes an affect, and sometimes a rhythm or a motor outline. The pathways of creativity are various, but limited in number. This variability in intuitive content determines three types of creativity, of which I have attempted to give examples in my book. Let us listen again to Valéry:

Noonday above, motionless Noonday
Thinking within itself and sufficient unto itself.

The third phase consists in this intuition of an image, a sensation, a movement, a psychic reality that is completely marginal, ex-centric, and unknown, transforming itself into a central nucleus from which or around which the work will be constructed, and in which it finds its point of departure or arrival. The topography of the mind turns inside out; what had been hidden, inert, and peripheral becomes an active germ, a luminous hearth, brain, womb. The capacity to make this inversion then becomes crucial. But what flesh is this nucleus going to sprout and flourish in? This is the problem of the choice of materials, not only that of material materials, like sounds, tubes of paint, marble, or words, but also of formal material: the form of the sonnet, the portrait, or the fugue. The work is embodied in these materials, its organizing code is made flesh: this is the work of the third phase.

The fourth phase will be the accomplishment in detail of this incarnation. This is composition properly so called:

What pure work of fine flashes consumes
Many diamonds that sparkle imperceptibly.

—work that takes place no longer at the unconscious level, but at the point where the preconscious and conscious meet. In a creator who has reached the years of maturity this involves dogged work and sustained labour, with many alterations, crossings-out, and variants. By contrast, in the thrust proper to juvenile creativity, it has been compared to a rapid, powerful, and barely controlled ejaculation and to a continuous outpouring, whose result wants to be perfect straight away.

Finally, the fifth movement comes along. The creator takes the difficult and arbitrary decision that his work is finished and exhibitable to a public.

Fly away, you completely dazzled pages,

cried Valérie on the point of finishing his 'La Cimetière marin'. It is an arbitrary decision, because one can always re-work the work, perfect it, complete it, and take it in hand again. What is more, modern aesthetics demand that a work remain fundamentally unfinished, as happened to Pascal with his *Pensées*, and like the theory that Umberto Eco put forward in *L'oeuvre ouverte*. In psychological terms the problem is as follows: to accept that the baby is leaving one's belly; to envisage that what one has conceived and carried can proceed to lead a life of its own. This gives rise to such resistances that many artists prefer to shelve their works, unhang their canvasses on the eve of varnishing them, destroy their films, or prohibit the publication of their writings, rather than take that risk.

These are the five moments of creativity. I have presented them in the most classic succession. One could define very different types of creativity on the basis of various possible combinations of these five elements. If my theory is relevant, it could be useful to others with this in mind.

GT: Where did you ultimately derive these five stages from?

DA: From several sources, which turned out to be convergent: from my own experience and the efforts I made in
the direction of literary creativity; from the study I devoted
to Freud's self-analysis (two volumes, P.U.F., 1975; English
trans., London: Karnac Books, 1986), drawing on his own
dreams, which he analysed and published in the form of
scattered fragments, but which are easy to date, combine,
and interpret, and which allow us to follow the progress of his
creative psychic work step by step whilst he was in the midst
of discovering psychoanalysis; finally, from creative artists'
intimate diaries, letters, theoretical writings, confidences
—though most give a watered-down, idealized, intellec-
tualized, or complacent version of what went on in them. If
they had been too conscious of it, they would have created
nothing. But some writers have been attentive to it; they
have registered in their preconscious their personal experience of the various phases of creativity, and they have transposed them into passages or characters in their works, ones
whose effect is precisely the strongest upon the public: I have
found in this an essential confirmation of the theses I propose. Each of these five moments turns out to be represented,
not necessarily in the same order or in the same work, but
sometimes here, sometimes there. For example, one of the
characters in the novel suffers a state of seizure, which is
that experienced by the creator at the moment when he
discovered the intuition that guided his story. It even happens that certain works have no other content than a transposition of the five phases of creative work, experienced
simultaneously by the author. I have suggested interpreting
one of the most constructed and commentated texts in
French literature in this light, Paul Valéry's 'La Cimetière
marin', by showing that this poem related, collected
together, assembled, and synthesized the five moments of
poetic creativity as Valéry himself experienced them when,
returning to the art of verse, he set about composing 'La
jeune Parque' between 1915 and 1917. 'Le Cimetière marin'

is his treatise both on aesthetics and on his poïetic art. With the help of this grid I have been able to offer a new interpretation of 'Le Cimetière marin'. The lines I have just quoted from it help in understanding it.

GT: It is something like this that Edgar Morin tried to do with his *Journal d'un livre*. But one has to be very strong to succeed in talking about one's own creative process, and to relate the process of birth of one's book. And it does not always yield the expected results. . . .

DA: If it is done in the form of a diary it can seem very narcissistic, too much are-you-looking-at-me. Valéry's strength lies in having conceived out of this experience a poem that is constructed according to rules of the most extreme formal rigour: twenty-four stanzas of six decasyllabic verses, with alternating masculine and feminine rhymes, and so forth. This austere form allowed him to sum up the experience of creativity with an astonishing and fascinating concision.

GT: You are drawn towards the experimental side of contemporary literature. It is striking to see that the authors that interest you, that you read with pleasure and comment upon in your essays on poïetics, are authors who belong to what has been called the *nouveau roman*. You were talking about Balzac a little while ago, and Flaubert, who are monuments, and nonetheless you said that they bore you. . . .

DA: I would not have the least desire to undertake a psychoanalytic study of Baudelaire, Flaubert, or Balzac. . . .

GT: Although Sartre harnessed himself to the task of performing psychoanalysis on Baudelaire, not to mention his Flaubert.

DA: Sartre's existential psychoanalysis rids itself too much of the unconscious; it is a distorted psychoanalysis. I do not want to say that his work on Baudelaire or Flaubert are without interest, but it is a mixture of phenomenology, sociology, and partial elements of psychoanalysis, rather one-sidedly slanted. Sartre seized upon that opportunity to reveal his own conscious and voluntarist experience of literary creativity, and at the same time to settle interminably his score with his family and milieu though the medium of authorship.

Having said that, it is true that the *nouveau roman* has interested me. Renouncing unity of plot and renouncing the omnipotent narrator who pulls the puppet strings of the characters and knows what is going on in them as the work proceeds seems to me to be closer to psychological truth. It seems to me to be enough to qualify as a writer if form is given to unconscious states and processes without their necessarily being attributed to characters who give the impression of being alive. But the form must be carefully crafted and as personal as its basis.

Psychoanalysis has had too much tendency to confine its approach to the content of the work, seen as the deployment of an unconscious phantasy that is at once personal and universal. It has not much studied form, genre, composition, and style. My first work of literary psychoanalysis, on obsessional discourse in the novels of Robbe-Grillet (which I reprinted in *Le Corps de l'oeuvre*), attempted precisely to draw a parallel between the author's stylistic techniques and these unconscious mechanisms of defence.

GT: Which authors have you done studies of?

DA: The horror of the void in Pascal, the figures of the depressive position in Julien Gracq, hallucination of the creative seizure in Henry James, Borges of course, and his acolyte Bioy Casares. Also Francis Bacon, painter of rents in the Skin Ego.

GT: Skin has been a great inspiration to painters, from the beauty of its texture in the nude to the torments that can be inflicted upon it.

DA: I met a painter from Anglet, between Biarritz and Bayonne, who in 1978 painted a picture representing a man dressing himself up in a woman's skin. Searching for a title, Charles Breuil wrote in succession on the back of his canvas:

Ta peau [your skin]
Ma peau [my skin]
Peau-Moi [skin-me]
PO
Moi-peau [me-skin; also Skin Ego]

And he finally settled upon 'The Envelope'. Naturally, he had never heard of my article on the Skin Ego in 1974. What a coincidence between an artist's intuition and a psycho-analyst's idea! It was only at the beginning of 1985 that we each discovered the other's work, thanks to a friend in common, J.-B. Ibar. We had a quite exceptional meeting together. Charles Breuil very kindly let me acquire his canvas. I have hung it in my consulting room, beside my analyst's armchair.

GT: To return to psychoanalytic literary criticism, have you any new projects?

DA: I would like to pay homage to the man that I regard as the greatest contemporary French writer (French and Irish), Samuel Beckett. In his youth he had a psychoanalysis with Bion in London. I am trying to define the influence that this concrete experience of psychoanalysis may have had upon his work, and what he transposed of it into his novels and short stories.

Ecology, anti-psychiatry, university

G T: M Anzieu, there is a subject that we have not yet touched upon, which is nevertheless very important, not only because it is much talked about, but, what is more, because in the years to come psychologists are going to devote attention to it together with sociologists. This is the problem of ecology and the environment. A multitude of specialists and experts from different disciplines have come together in different countries of the world to protest energetically and by every means at their disposal against the pollution of the environment that is literally raining down upon us, no matter what country we live in. Have psychologists in general adopted a position in relation to this problem? As a psychoanalyst, what do you yourself think about squandering energy and spreading pollution? You may say that that is a social problem, but psychoanalysts can also have views upon social problems. What is this self-destructiveness, conscious or unconscious, which means that the laws that exist in certain countries to protect the environment are in no way respected either by industry or by citizens in a fairly general way? It all seems as if people were sinking into sheer wantonness in a sort of collective suicide. Could you tell us what you think about this, as a citizen and as a psychoanalyst?

DA: One of my ambitions would be to take up and modernize Freud's work *Civilization and Its Discontents*, which appeared in 1930. In half a century this discontent has evolved; it persists and has perhaps strengthened, but its causes are different and so is its nature. Freud placed his emphasis upon sexual repression in the industrialized societies, which is no longer true today. To give you my opinion and outline conjectures rather than truly worked-out hypotheses, it seems to me that while human beings, thanks to scientific and technical progress, are mastering the manufacture of implements and objects as never before in the history of mankind, they are on the other hand experiencing a need to deliver attacks against external nature. The artificial passes for good and is appropriated; what is natural passes for bad and is attacked. Here there is a phenomenon of splitting in the Kleinian sense of the term. Anything that is fertile, strong, and intelligent in human beings is mobilized into production, its renewal, expansion, and refinement, and in its corollary, consumption. All of a sudden, aggressive instincts are found to be dissociated from the life instincts, but social and international competition is not sufficient to give them an outlet. So it is external nature that turns out to be hated, soiled, and mutilated, without the human beings taking note that in so doing it is their own natural base, physical and biological, that they are destroying.

GT: Is this a unique phenomenon in the history of mankind?

DA: I am not enough of a historian and anthropologist to know that. But it looks as though uncontrolled demographic expansion, pollution of the natural environment, the atomic menace, and a certain number of other factors besides—it all looks as though at the very moment mankind had arrived at the height of its technical power, it found itself disarmed when faced with its own self-destructive drive and was seeking to actualize it by the means that I have just mentioned. Here there is matter for psychoanalysts to think about.

GT: In France you have, among other things, the movement of Brice Lalonde, who has put forward an ecology programme and candidates since the last but one legislative elections. This is something new not only in France, but in many industrialized countries, like Germany with its 'Greens'. . . .

DA: Yes. What is more, I live in Paris in the 5th arrondissement, which is the constituency that Brice Lalonde stood for, and where there has been the strongest percentage of votes in favour of the ecologists.

GT: Indeed. But it is striking to see the extent to which this movement has scarcely caught on, subsequently and even at that time, because it did not even get the 5% of votes necessary to get the expenses of its electoral campaign reimbursed. On the one hand, you have a growing awareness, which started as usual with the intellectuals. On the other hand, the 'écolos', as you call them in France, have scarcely any following. Are they not perhaps seen as nutcases by most of the population?

DA: The French are becoming increasingly sensitized to ecological facts. I find this around me, as much in my family as in my neighbourhood or my relationships: a wish for pedestrian streets, a wish to protect green spaces, a wish to plant trees, a wish to have flowers in one's window, a wish to defend the countryside against the implantation of electricity pylons or concrete apartment blocks—all these little facts definitely show a growing sensitivity, and one that I believe is on the way to becoming a majority one, even if the traditional bipolarization of French political life between the Right and the Left puts a brake upon its expression.

For three quarters of a century psychoanalysis has been ecological before its time: giving time several times a week to a patient who lives in the hurly-burly outside his sessions, letting him speak when the means of mass communication are continually invading him with a flood of discourse, setting up an environment in which he feels listened to without being flattered, respected while being frustrated, and free from the danger of being contradicted; letting him speak, be silent, regress and progress at his own rhythmn, and letting him find a natural balance and not a forced or distorted one—is that not a micro-ecology?

GT: M Anzieu, you are probably not a specialist in what is called in France institutional psychotherapy, with François Tosquelles, Fernand Oury, or Aïda Vasquez. You have, however, read the work of Cooper and Laing on anti-psychiatry: I am thinking especially of Cooper's *The Death of the Family*. I am also thinking of the work of Roger Gentis, especially the one that deals with the walls of the asylum. Without being an expert in these areas, because you have not worked directly in a psychiatric setting either continuously or full-time, could you all the same give us your opinion about these movements, these theses, and this philosophy? Is it true, for example, that the seriously mentally ill, the psychotic, have more chance of being cured—given that one is never really cured of a psychosis or a schizophrenia (I recall that Bruno Bettelheim wrote in *The Empty Fortress* that his life would be a success if he managed to cure a single schizophrenic—which is a huge claim, if you know Bruno Bettelheim)—is it true that psychotics have a greater chance of being reinserted into life, of being able at least to function in a socially acceptable manner, if they are cared for outside the walls of mental hospitals rather than inside them? Or, to put it another way, will not the walls of mental hospitals shut in psychotics for ever?

DA: Here you are raising the problem of chronicization. I have followed the beginning of the movement for institutional psychotherapy with great interest. I regularly found Tosquelles on study days at the Société française de Psychothérapie de Groupe. We had shared interests in psychodrama and group methods—I in my own area of formation and personal therapy, and he in his area of action on and in institutions: there we had points of convergence and agreement. I also followed the late Georges Daumezon's initiatives in the field of sociotherapy, giving the mentally ill group activities that would lead them out of their pathological withdrawal, help them develop interactions among themselves and with objects in reality, proceed to libidinal recharge, and alleviate the destructive hatred of reality that characterizes them. I share Oury's opinion on a point that Tosquelles had in fact already made—namely, that psychiatric institutions must be caring. It is not only the doctors, psychologists, nurses, and teachers that have to be caring—the institution as such has to be caring. And to begin with, it must not be allowed to be pathogenic.

GT: Whereas at the present time psychiatric institutions are pathogenic in Western countries—not to speak of course of psychiatric institutions in certain Eastern countries, which are pathogenic in a different way by putting themselves at the service of power and the repression of political dissidents with the help of chemical drugs.

DA: The institution must be *caring* in the English sense of the word, which includes medical treatment just as much as the ongoing care of the type given by a mother to a baby, and it must be so towards the caring staff themselves as much as towards patients. The few concrete researches that I have been able to conduct in group and institutional psycho-analysis by means of creating a positive group atmosphere notably with the help of psychodrama mean that I feel I have a certain affinity at that level with institutional psycho-therapy.

GT: In that case, you certainly have reservations at other levels.

DA: I am not in agreement when claims are made to abol-ish the difference between cared for and carer, and when one can no longer tell when one meets someone in a caring institution whether he is a patient or a therapist. This is not good for either party. What I have found in individual and group psychoanalytic work is that distinctions of this sort in their turn allow differentiations internal to the psychic apparatus to be established, which enrich and improve its functioning. In trying to suppress fundamental distinctions in order to cure certain psychic disorders one creates others. Another point on which I am not in agreement is about a utopia that has developed from anti-psychiatry: the utopia of believing that the patient would not be ill if his social, profes-sional, and family environment would support him and treat him with understanding. Certainly we must, as far as pos-sible, not separate the child from his parents, nor the ill person from his family, and we must try to treat the latter as a whole. But there exist very young children whose baffling reactions drive their mother mad, and adult psychotics who try to draw their male or female companion into their delu-sion or suicide. It is too easy to blame society or family relationships. Finally, one last point that you yourself have mentioned. Certain proponents of anti-psychiatry are con-tributing to the spread of the illusion that all mental ill-nesses can be cured. You have just reminded us of what Bettelheim said. Improvements are possible; one can prevent

crises and decompensations that would render the psychic
state of certain persons irreversible. But one cannot change
the deep structures of a psychic personality. One can help a
person to live with this structure; one can offer him adjustments, ways of compensating for his deficiencies, a better
adaptation to reality and other people, and the art of avoiding situations that would risk touching him on his vulner-
able points and provoking decompensation in a deluded,
hallucinatory, or self-destructive mode.

GT: M Anzieu, I would like to ask you a delicate question. I
remember that when we met for the first time to discuss this
project for a joint book, you said to me, half seriously and half
in jest, 'In this book, I feel I shall be able to tell you *everything*.' You used that expression—and, I do not know why,
but I immediately associated it with the problem of hierarchy in French universities. I said to myself, 'Didier Anzieu
has therefore not been able to say everything about his
intellectual progress at certain moments in his life, and he
has had to wait not only for success, but for the summit of his
career for there no longer to be any fear of the institution and
for him at last to be able to *tell everything*.' Why could you not
'tell everything' earlier? What can you now say that you
could not have said before?

DA: I consider myself able to say everything where I have
something serious to say. I have replied to some of your
questions in a lateral, superficial, or partial way because I
had nothing better to say to you. I have the sense that I have
formulated everything that I think and that seems to me to
be based in the books and articles that I have published, in
talks I have given, and in the conversations we have had
together; I do not feel that an important, crucial, essential
idea remains unspoken. Unless it be what remains and will
no doubt remain hidden of my unconscious. Also excluded is
what concerns my private life, for this is not relevant to
readers of this type of work. As for the danger—which is

inevitable in the sort of interviews we are having—of expos-
ing myself personally and having to tolerate criticism, com-
plaints, and attacks, I accept this, I think, without excessive
anxiety or vanity. Is not relative wisdom an attribute of the
age that I have reached?

GT: In the French university to which you belong, with its
excessively hierarchical structure, can a young senior lecturer or a young lecturer advance with impunity into territory occupied by his elders? Even if he is original, brilliant,
and creative, can he get going with impunity, without taking
precautions, and without having definite support within an
almost military hierarchy? Indeed, the University has often
been compared with the army. . . .

DA: I find you harsh.

GT: Nonetheless, these are slogans that were vaunted in
May 1968, in France!

DA: By students who had not done military service!

GT: Let us say that I exaggerate, but there is certainly a
stifling hierarchy in the French universities. . . .

DA: Hierarchy is one issue, and the possibility or impos-
sibility of speaking is another, for I have known non-hier-
archized systems in which it was impossible to say what one
wanted to say, and I have known—in 1968, at Nanterre—a
hierarchized university that was very liberal and let students say anything.

GT: If you were at the Ministry of Education in France, and
if you were given the Universities portfolio, what kinds of
reforms would you make?

DA: I have for a long time been satisfied with the French universities. I was satisfied as a student, I was satisfied as a lecturer, but I am less and less satisfied as a professor—not because the university stops me from saying what I have to say, for I have always been able to say what I have had to say by using the proper forms and choosing the opportune moment. I have been more or less listened to, more or less accepted, but I have always found at the University, first of all teachers, then colleagues, students, and collaborators, in whom what I have had to say met an echo. In their turn, my colleagues and students have made no bones about coming to me, to tell me things that have enlightened me, that have sometimes made me change my views or attitude, and sometimes to oppose me quite openly. What I regret about the French universities are their lack of material means, and their climb-down in the face of the problem of selection, which is nonetheless necessary. We are swamped by an excessive number of ill-prepared and poorly motivated students, who later have the greatest difficulty in finding openings and making the best of them.

GT: French universities have been taxed with being too abstract and Cartesian, with forming beautiful minds, but ones that are lost as soon as they leave the university precinct or womb. Students have many difficulties in entering the world of whatever kind of work, for the good reason that they have lived for years in a sort of temple or cloud in which the reign of ideas and concepts was such that they very often lost touch with reality, whereas American universities are much more pragmatic and involve students in society during the course of university education itself.

DA: If I were responsible for the reform of higher education—but I warn you straight away that what I would propose would never be accepted—I would demand that higher studies *had* to be done half-time; that is, no one could be a student for half his year or half of his day unless for the other half he had practical work. And this practical work should ultimately be remunerated and allow him to earn his living and finance his studies: this point, although not negligible, seems to me to be a side issue. The primary objective would be to put the future functionaries of the nation in contact with a concrete activity, as well as with social realities, to make them learn the discipline of work, and to make them discover that one does not work alone, but with others, within an organization or a collective plan.

GT: I would draw your attention to the fact that this is in fact increasingly going on in North America. Most students work part-time—in the summer, for example, or in their free time, when they have any. They are in fact very integrated into social and professional life. This is a North American measure: would you recommend it?

DA: I heard Khrushchev propose it in the Soviet Union when he came into power. Nowadays, with unemployment and the economic crisis, there can be no question either of imposing a professional activity upon students or of introducing selection for entry to university, for a quite simple reason: in France, universities hold back access to the world of work for about 300,000 young people every year. This means the government, whether of the Right or of the Left, has one less thing to worry about. Alteration in the political majority has changed nothing on this point. It is not within my competence to find out how this serious and painful problem of unemployment might be resolved, but I do think that to ask the universities to assume an economic function as a priority would be to pervert their fundamental vocation of teaching and research. My natural reserve where what one calls politics is concerned has been reinforced by what I have seen in the course of the various duties I have had to discharge as president of a certain number of scientific associations, as head of department, and as one of the assistants of the president of my university. It has often seemed to me that the given facts of situations in which we found ourselves imposed certain logical solutions, and did so independently of any political consideration, whereas colleagues and students prevented the effective solution being retained because they calculated that it would benefit or disadvantage one or other political party. Some even maintained that it would be better to allow the situation to get as bad as possible, because then a lovely disturbance would ensue, which would make a clean sweep of what exists and make anything possible. No one, of course, had the least idea what they meant by this 'anything'. In this way I have seen useful measures and necessary reforms postponed indefinitely, by putting off what it would have been more sound and effective to do straight away until a morrow that never comes. I have unfortunately witnessed, for this and some other reasons, a reduction in the quality of French universities, and I remain very affected by it.

Return to May 1968
and to groups

G T: In July 1968 you published with Éditions Fayard under the pseudonym Épistémon (why Épistémon? Because of epistemology?) a book that is today out of print, entitled *Ces idées qui ont ébranlé la France* [These Ideas That Have Shaken France]. In it you gave your version of the events of May 1968 in France. Many did that; Touraine did it, Edgar Morin did it—everyone wrote their own little book, their little breviary, their little interpretation of May 1968. Could you, for the readers who have not read the book, tell us first of all why you published it under a pseudonym? It is the first time that you used one. . . .

DA: Absolutely.

GT: And why this pseudonym in particular? And could you at the same time describe briefly what your own interpretation of the events of May 1968 contributed, because I suppose that the psychoanalyst Anzieu evaluated this situation somewhat differently from the sociologists who called themselves Touraine or Morin?

DA: The events of May 1968 had their origin at the University of Nanterre, where I had been professor since its opening four years previously and where I had founded and directed the department of psychology. I would like to recall the names of the twelve other first professors who were appointed from 1 October 1964, each to organize the teaching of their speciality: Arnavon (civilization of the English-speaking countries), Beaujeu (Latin), Blanc (Geography), Crouzet (History), D'Hangest (English language and literature), Mlle Duchemin (Greek), Dufrenne (Philosophy), Grappin (German), who was our Doyen, Micha (Old French literature), Michaud (Contemporary French literature), Pottier (Spanish), and Vernière (Modern French literature). The thirteen of us, in the desert space available for cultivation that was afforded by this close Paris suburb, were united by a heroic mentality, a pioneering ideal, facing the antique, decrepit, and narrow Sorbonne, which was suffocating itself in the centre of Paris. We considered ourselves the council of gods of a new Olympus, the twelve apostles of a new University, grouped around our Doyen, who was spreading the good word and who was going to end his career at Nanterre betrayed, vilified, and morally crucified. Without our enthusiasm, our openness, our reformism, our liberal spirit, and without our marginality in relation to the City and tradition, I think that nothing in particular would have happened at the University of Nanterre. I was therefore an immediate witness of the first part of the events.

At this university, the explosion happened in May 1968, but it had been preceded, since November and December 1967, by a certain number of incidents in the courses, including my own, on the university campus, or at the opening of the stadium and swimming pool—incidents that were alarm signals that we did not understand, but that heralded what was about to happen. Having been caught up from the beginning in the event and its development, I experienced the need to write what I felt and to do so while it was fresh. Besides, this was an exercise for which I had training, through my experience of conducting formation groups in which one attempted *while it was fresh* to communicate to the group what one felt about what was going on and in which, in the interval between sessions, I always take notes on what I have understood, on the hypotheses I am making, and about what I am going to say or what I have said.

GT: However, M Anzieu, it was not a small group at Nanterre, as you would agree. You, who were saying in a previous interview that you had a horror of—the word is too strong—large groups and crowds, here you were all the same surveying a crowd (and not a demonstration by a small group); in fact you analysed a movement that far exceeded anything that could take place in a small formation group.

DA: I protest. I only dealt with what went on at Nanterre. When subsequently in June the movement spread to the Sorbonne and the rest of the French universities, I learned of it through the newspapers and radio, but I did not feel I had any further competence to say anything at all about it. It was the detonating moment that interested me, and it is always the moment of coming unstuck that interests me, as much in my research on literary creativity as in group psychology: the moment of crisis, and what comes out of it. At the beginning at Nanterre it was a small group phenomenon. The movement took shape and developed out of several small groups of students. There were anarchists, Trotskyites, Maoists, situationists. . . .

GT: Which you had known well at the University of Strasburg, where the latter movement began. . . .

DA: I maintain that the agitation gained body because at the beginning small groups were involved. At Nanterre throughout the whole of the winter of 1967–1968 these little groups provoked intermittent actions, which created an atmosphere of crisis—that is, they threw into crisis traditional values, the style of teaching, the mode of nomination of professors, the definition of programmes, and the concept of examinations. On 22 March 1968 a symbolic and federative action took place. Some students climbed to the top of the administrative tower that dominates the campus, which they regarded as a phallic emblem, symbol of the administrative power of the Doyen and the intellectual power of the professors. At the top there was, and there still is, the Council room, which was then reserved for professors. Representatives of each of these small groups occupied this room to prevent the professors from holding their meeting. They spent the night there, they held discussions among themselves, they federated themselves, and they created a group of delegates of these groups, which called itself 'the Movement of the 22nd of March' and which took in hand the development of the situation. This was an intermediate group between the small and the large group. But this still remained in the area of groups; we were not yet into the crowd, nor into the mass. To take up an expression that Serge Moscovici used a lot, what was involved was an active minority, who transformed the climate of the passive mass of students and the traditional grouping of the teaching body. In my book I tried to explain how such a group phenomenon was able in its turn to trigger off a mass phenomenon. I do not feel competent to interpret the subsequent development proper to this mass phenomenon—how it was taken over by the Unions, the C.G.T., and the political parties. As an individual I did not take part in it; as a psychologist, it went beyond my explanatory register. It was simply the creative moment that interested me.

GT: How did you interpret this creative moment?

DA: Before passing on my interpretation to you, I would like to make it clear that the teaching body at Nanterre was torn apart by these events, because it was a new faculty in which the teaching was at once very solid and very modern, and contact with the students was simple and easy. We were all, I repeat, liberals, partisans of social evolution and pedagogic evolution. I had put into practice methods of training students in psychology through group dynamics and psychodrama, for example. We had the bitter surprise of finding that where pedagogy had remained reactionary, the students stayed inert and did not react; whereas here, on the contrary, where we had taken a step towards them, they were falling upon us. The majority of my colleagues at Nanterre could not understand the explosion of May 1968 at all. They had forgotten that the century of Enlightenment had produced the French Revolution. And who was it that made the greatest effort to understand? The historians and psychologists—the two categories of researchers who in their own areas were accustomed to take crises into consideration. One cannot do history without attending to political, economic, and social crises, and one cannot do psychology, especially after Freud, without taking psychic conflict into consideration, and the crises that punctuate the evolution of every individual life. We were witnessing a crisis that, in its nascent state, possessed both a socio-political dimension and a psychological dimension. 'It' spoke to us psychologists and historians; 'it' questioned us, 'it' canvassed us, 'it' irritated us, and 'it' excited us. The events of May–June 1968 and their repercussions, which occupied us for years, were one of the most exciting experiences that I have had. I had already lived intensely through certain group experiences, especially the pedagogic training seminar for officers posted to the Capital during the Algerian war, which I have already alluded to.

The events at Nanterre were for me an experience of a spontaneous and involuntary group seminar, which deeply touched and unsettled me. I tried to understand, and I wanted to translate this understanding immediately into a book. You asked me about the pseudonym. The work was due out in mid-July 1968. There was no way of knowing how the movement would turn out. For myself, I wanted to remain present and active in my university as Anzieu, without necessarily being marked by what I was able to write. I needed to make a distinction between Anzieu the professor, active in his place of teaching, and Anzieu the group psychoanalyst, reflecting upon what was going on. I took the pseudonym Épistémon. It was not I who chose that. The publisher who commissioned this book suggested the name, which is that of a character in Rabelais. The event that was shaking France had taken on a Rabelaisian aspect, and Épistémon wants to be 'he who knows'.

GT: For the first time it seems that you were somewhat afraid of signing a book in your own name?

DA: Listen. I think that my principal reason was that as an analyst continuing to have patients in individual treatment I owed it to myself to preserve in me a certain image of neutrality so as to guarantee the people who consulted me the minimum of necessary internal security.

GT: All the same, you did publish your *Contes à rebours* in your own name.

DA: Yes, but this other issue came several years later. Let me remind you of the succession of events. I published on Nanterre under a pseudonym. This pseudonym was quickly seen through and revealed, and the press made haste to say who was hiding behind it. I then saw that this book was far from costing me the difficulties that I had feared (with respect to some of my distant colleagues, yes, it did cost me difficulties), but where my students and my closest colleagues were concerned, it gained me a strengthened esteem, even among those who did not share all my opinions in matters of university action. Notably, the book was of use to M Edgar Faure who had just been nominated Minister of National Education, and to all his cabinet. They withdrew, also in a seminar during the summer of 1968, for a whole week to prepare what was to be the law of university orientation, and it was principally Michel de Certeau's book on the liberation of speech and mine—the point of view of a group psychoanalyst—that they used for inspiration. And when the universities reopened in November 1968, M Edgar Faure suggested I be commissioned at his cabinet to promote a status of psychologist, which was lacking in France. I accepted, and for five months I fought in vain for this project, which was finally promulgated seventeen years later in 1985. This showed that it did no harm to my teaching activity to have used the pseudonym, nor to have had it swiftly unveiled. It did no harm either to my work as an analyst in my consulting room. When the problem arose afresh of publishing personal texts, namely my *Contes à rebours* seven years later, I first of all had the idea of taking a new pseudonym. In my daydreams I entertained an omnipotent phantasy of being several characters who would each create a different work. This was before Romain Gary set the example with his novels attributed to Émil Ajar. I expected to give myself a series of pseudonyms—one for fiction, another for essays, a third for a fantastic biography, and so forth. And then, reflecting that my pseudonym Épistémon had not been an impediment, and that I even seemed a bit absurd for having wanted to give myself a pseudonym, I decided to speak, write, and publish in my own name.

GT: Let us return to the interpretation that you gave of the events of May 1968.

DA: Apart from the demographic and socio-cultural causes (the massive increase in the number of students in the industrialized societies), which inevitably interested me as a teacher but about which I had no original thoughts to present, what struck me was the influence of certain ideas. That is why my book was entitled *Ces idées qui ont ébranlé la France*. Among them, those of Jean-Paul Sartre in *The Critique of Dialectical Reason* (which appeared in 1960) held my attention in so far as this philosophical work was also a book on groups. He showed exactly how movements that transform society arise out of small red-hot groups that spread like wild-fire and create a particular state of mind, the *riot*, which is apt to dissolve stale traditional values and to produce an experience that renews liberty, equality, and fraternity.

GT: This is more than philosophy—it is sociology.

DA: It is a philosophical reflection. Sartre started off from the work of the American psycho-sociologist Kurt Lewin, whom he criticized, and he proposed a whole philosophy of history on the basis of his interpretation of the days of July 1789 in Paris. Sartre objected to the artificial stakes of their experimental groups in the work of psycho-sociologists, whereas there, in July 1789, as in May 1968, something vital, which was at once individual and collective, was at stake. I therefore tried to show, at a time when the structuralists held intellectual power, with Lacan, Foucault, Lévi-Strauss, and other Bartheses, how the days of May 1968 had ensured the triumph of existentialism over them. I even wrote a little passage on the death of structuralism, which earned me a part in a debate that occupied two pages in the newspaper *Le Monde*: 'For or against structuralism'. It seemed to me that in Sartre, and in the theoreticians of groups in general, there were ideas that were proving to be active agents upon social dynamics, whereas structural analyses offered keys for understanding individual and social history after the event but were inoperative when faced with a concrete event like this.

GT: When you speak of structuralism, you do not mention that of Goldmann, who did try to juxtapose structure and history in his genetic structuralism.

DA: I knew and appreciated Lucien Goldmann. His theme of the tragic vision of the world seemed important to me. His work on Pascal's *Pensées* is excellent. But I would situate Goldmann at the side of Sartre rather than Lévi-Strauss, Foucault, Althusser, and Barthes. I was therefore struck by the crisis of identity that the events of 1968 revealed among the young men and women of societies that were industrialized or on the way to industrialization. Analogous movements had already appeared abroad (in China and at the University of California at Berkeley), and they were widespread between 1968 and 1970 in the universities of numerous countries. This crisis of personal identity among the young has broken out all over the world, independently of political régimes, because industrial civilization no longer guarantees young people a place, a future, or a *raison d'être* and plunges them into a surfeit of knowledge and a void of cultural models—whence the development of a utopia among students, which I tried to analyse, and one of whose functions seemed to me to be to deny how unbearable this new form of social reality was for them. In that situation, young people developed group imaginings that became by contagion social imaginings, concerning the automatic right for all those who wanted it to studies, diplomas, and opportunities; and also concerning a transformation of society that could only be radical. In a sense we were present experimentally at the birth of a utopia, not invented and dictated by an original researcher in the isolation of his study, but one that developed day by day in group discussions and through collective speech. This experience of collective creation of a social utopia doubly fascinated me, as citizen and as psychoanalyst, and I tried to analyse it by relating it to the conditions in which young people found themselves at that particular moment. Reflecting upon it further and with hindsight, I have cherished the idea of rewriting my book; I even signed a contract with the publisher for a new edition rounded off by a second section, to be entitled, 'Nanterre, ten years later'. I began to work on it. But in 1978, for the tenth anniversary of the events, there was such an inflation in publications about May 1968 that I was loath to contribute to this intellectual overkill. I contented myself with including a supplementary chapter in the second edition of my book *Le Groupe et l'inconscient* (Dunod, 1981), which developed the new point of view that I had to add. Historians of religion, notably Jean-Pierre Vernant in his study of ancient Greek religion, show that tragedy in Greece only functioned for one century, from the middle of the fifth century to the middle of the fourth century BC. Why neither earlier nor later? It is because tragedy, according to Vernant, was a staging and dramatization through the intermediary of heroes of a crucial conflict between traditional values inherited from the ancient Hellenic monarchies and the rising values that conveyed a new conception of the cosmos, the city, and man. Tragedy represents the resistance of the characters *in situ* in the name of ancient beliefs that are on the point of extinction, and of their pitiless, bloody, pathetic struggle against the new beliefs that are called upon to take the lead, but at the price of sacrifice, and killing a hero, too much before his time. Once the new ideas had triumphed, tragedy no longer had a *raison d'être*, and it gave way to other genres. It has seemed to me that the events of May 1968 were a tragedy in modern guise, not written in advance, but spontaneous, and with a series of psychodramas instead of episodes, that ended up by turning into sociodrama. . . .

GT: People even spoke of a 'happening'. . . .

DA: Yes, of happenings whose multiplication and succession produced effects equivalent to those that tragedy produced among the fifth-century Greeks. My analysis was confirmed by the fact that the political stirrings of May 1968 were virtually cancelled out there and then, because a government of the Right remained in power and a Chamber of Deputies with an absolute Gaullist majority was elected. Economic life was only slightly modified. By contrast, the change in lifestyle was radical, in areas such as the conquest of sexual freedom by young people, the right to abortion and contraception, a more liberal attitude, more tolerance towards homosexuality; more direct relations between professors and students, a greater simplicity in communication between persons, and the rise of demands for self-determination and ecological hopes. The field was open for anyone to speak who wanted to. Where previously speech had only been repressed or not listened to, it became possible to be heard. Here is the interpretation that I now give of these events: a mutation of ideas and social attitudes came about under the impact of this dramatization in innumerable small groups of the conflict between old and new values.

GT: Would you say that we have witnessed a rupture in lifestyle?

DA: René Kaës, several colleagues, and I have entitled a book *Crise, rupture et dépassement* (Dunod, 1979), in which we show how every crisis provokes ruptures with old equilibria at the risk of depression and decompensation in individuals and leads to a search for new methods and new objectives, so long as a 'transitional' space is made between the old state and the new one.

GT: However, many political observers describe France as having scarcely evolved since May 1968.

DA: This is because outside the universities and the intellectual élites there has been a great fear, one analogous to Mediaeval fears of witchcraft, famine, plague, and other epidemics—fears that certainly correspond to dangerous realities, but which, because of the social imaginings that they trigger off, are out of all proportion with reality itself. The fear that followed upon May 1968 therefore led to a strengthening and hardening of political power, which was nonetheless sufficiently skilful to use for its own advantage everything from the propositions of May 1968 that seemed salvageable from it. A strong power is a protection against fear. But equally there were blunders by those who set themselves up as leaders of the movement of May 1968. Among these I knew Cohn-Bendit: he was one of my students. He interrupted some of my courses. He was a remarkable debater. But they were surprised to have power at their disposal. They had criticized it so much. . . .

GT: . . . that they no longer knew what to do with it, once they had got it . . .

DA: That's it. They did not know what to do with it. The trade unions took up the movement that was under way, but without themselves daring to exercise power either. De Gaulle had packed his bags and gone to Baden-Baden; he was doubtless expecting the Elysée to be taken by storm and a new power to be installed. The pattern of the days of 1789 (I mentioned a little while ago Jean-Paul Sartre's analysis) was ripe for reproduction. But no Bastille was taken. There had, indeed, been the rather symbolic and ephemeral seizure of the administrative tower at Nanterre, and in Paris the Odéon had been taken, but this remained in the theatrical domain. Seizure of the Elysée or of the National Assembly were put off *sine die* to morrows that never came. I do not know whether nature has a horror of a vacuum, but every society and every institution has a horror of the absence of power. If those who had provoked this absence did not quickly occupy power, they ultimately left its old tenants in place.

GT: So power was only taken symbolically. . . .

DA: Not even that. It was only taken in imagination. Indeed, the formula written on walls was 'Power to the imagination'. I attended excited and exciting discussions among my students and colleagues: now that we had power, we were going to change teaching, to reform methods, objectives, and programmes. I agreed with all that, but it was very quickly denounced as belonging to a reformist perspective. The 'revolutionary' ultra-left wanted to bring about total destruction in order to be able to construct a new society in which there would be room for a new university, and when one asked them which, they replied that one would see that clearly enough when it was being built. You cannot make plans in advance, they said, because to anticipate would already be to impose, and therefore to appropriate a new power to oneself. But by refusing any form of power, they fell into helplessness. They hurled words about instead of taking the action that would have been necessary. Their influence upon students at the beginning of the academic year, in October 1968 and in the winter of 1968–69, crumbled and fell away because they had nothing concrete or realizable to propose. Raymond Aron's book presenting the opposite point of view to mine then came out with the same publisher, Fayard: *La Révolution introuvable* [The Undiscoverable Revolution]. It ridiculed this pseudo-revolution that had taken power and done nothing with it. These ultra-leftists were, what is more, dubbed 'Mao-Spontex': Mao for their cultural reference, and Spontex, which is the name of a brand of sponge, because of their spontaneism: they were sponges that absorbed anything, but without any consistency.

GT: That verges upon political irresponsibility. . . .

DA: Be that as it may, the Right did not fail to make denunciations to its own advantage. There has been a collision between the Great Fear of thinkers of fine thoughts and this juvenile irresponsibility. At depth, what had interested the disputants of May 1968 was to work on a utopia together, and not a practical project.

GT: This is Marcuse.

DA: Yes.

GT: However, today one still finds a world-wide swerve to the right. [It should be remembered that this was written in 1985.] Reagan is enthroned in the United States. It is little better in the Soviet Union; the whole world now knows what a so-called popular democracy can mean when there is not only what Solzhenitsyn has revealed to us about the gulags, but what many other dissidents have come to tell us about the ways in which the rights of man are unrecognized there; it is also a military imperialism, albeit thoroughly Communist. So, on one side it is said: here is this youth, which had demonstrated in favour of these gigantic 'happenings', not only in France, but in California, Italy, Spain, and Germany, and almost everywhere in the world. Then, on the other hand, when one looks at the political structures that surround them, one notices this visible political hardening. So here we have two weights and two measures: we talk of juvenile and post-juvenile effervescence, which goes off in all directions and gives at first sight the impression of a liberation of energies and libido; on the other hand, one sees to what extent this libido and energy are in reality locked up and held in check by iron shackles, if only one analyses them.

DA: All the same, freedom of lifestyle, short skirts, the lowering of the age of majority, free access to publications and erotic films, the right to homosexuality, the possibility for each to live their sexuality as he or she pleases, so long as they do no violence to one another, the fact of not being able to beget children without the agreement of both partners, and many other things as well—all of this is tending to spread to the whole world, whatever the nature of its political régime. Since May 1968 a new event has intervened: the world energy crisis. In 1968 we were in the midst of economic expansion, full employment was *de rigueur*, unemployment was unknown, and the forward progress of production, consumption, and revenues was regular from one year to the next. Young people could therefore entertain a wish to study for free, with the automatic reward of a diploma, and with work thereafter in which there would be the least constraints possible, and which would allow them to continue to cultivate themselves freely. Since the socio-economic context has changed, young people have felt their wings to be clipped. Imagination has lost its power over them; the realities that disturb them are unemployment, drugs, the difficulty and fragility of loving relationships, and the pitiless selection that professional life exercises upon individuals. In France, the new generations of students for whom May 1968 means nothing because they were children then are dull, studious, and co-operative, and they lack a taste for collective festivity.

GT: Perhaps it would be good on the basis of the experience of Nanterre, but without confining yourself to it, if you could explain to us how your psychoanalytic work with groups differs from sociological action, as you described it in your book about May 1968, and from so-called wild group analysis; these are notions with which readers are not always very familiar. Could you put us in the picture about that and tell us how psychologists differ from sociologists when they take groups?

DA: Certain colleagues put techniques of group dynamics at the service of political or ideological options. They use group phenomena like collective detonators that trigger off disputes in the institutions in which they are intervening, or even like instruments for permanent social destabilization.

For me, the aim of group methods, like that of individual psychoanalysis, is to permit a subject—here, a group—to grasp the meaning of its deep desire and to put itself in the best practical conditions to fulfil this desire in action and work, not in dreams. As for this desire, it is not up to me to pass judgement upon it, whether as group leader or as psychoanalyst. I do not intervene in basic matters. I have observed that certain colleagues, as soon as a group began to take a direction that did not correspond with their personal ideology, put pressure on them to make them change their minds. They no longer applied themselves to listening to the group but made the group listen to them.

GT: They not only manipulated them, but they exercised their functions more to satisfy their taste for power than to serve the objectives of the group.

DA: They would reply that groups themselves are influenced by the social and political climate in which they live and from which they must be helped to detach themselves. In fact, they set themselves up as judges of a certain truth. They do not allow the group to be its own source of its truth.

GT: It would perhaps be good to distinguish the different types of groups that you lead: therapeutic groups to which individuals come for treatment and formation groups to which they come not only to understand themselves better, but to reflect together about what they want.

DA: I have proposed the following formulation to distinguish them: in the first case, the participants want to stop suffering without having to change; in the second case, they would like to change without having to suffer.

GT: You obviously do not use the same technique. In a therapeutic group, your interventions are mainly centred

upon individuals. In a formation group or during an intervention in a going concern you work upon the very constitution of the group, and upon the trials it will have to undergo
to reach its autonomy as a group.

DA: When I use group methods, whatever their aim, I
always address myself to the group, and it is always group
phenomena that I make efforts to understand as a priority. In
a therapeutic group, I always link an interpretation aimed at
one person to an interpretation concerning the rest of the
group. A group forms a sounding-box for the various individual phantasies and psychic conflicts. It is a resonant phenomenon, like in acoustics or electromagnetism. But whereas we
have been able to establish the laws of physical resonance,
we have only been able to describe the types of psychological
resonance. All the same, the concept is precious to us. A
group forms in the first instance when the phantasies of
several individuals begin to resonate with one another;
secondly, when its members mobilize a shared defensive
system against this phantastic resonance; and, thirdly, when
the group elaborates compromise formations, as René Kaës
has shown, in the form of shared imaginary representations
of a mythical or ideological or utopian nature. It is on these
collective productions that the group psychoanalyst works.
Group members can find themselves touched or improved by
the operation of two mechanisms: by the knock-on effect of
the work done upon the group formations with which he has
entered into resonance, and because each of the group members tends to function at one moment or another as co-thera-
pist towards the person whose psychological problems have
become the most acute. Psychoanalytic work on the group,
therefore, has indirect effects upon the individuals. From
this point of view my general method remains the same
whatever the aim: therapeutic, formative, or help to a real
group that has been paralysed by its internal problems. By
contrast, it is obvious that when the processes and aims are

different, the techniques of interpretation will be different.

GT: I have myself attempted to do some research, by relating participants' interventions (according to Bales's twelve categories) to what is going on in the groups in order to try to identify a kind of group structure as far as possible. [See G. Tarrab, 'Quels sont les comportements les plus propices pour assumer des positions de leadership dans les groupes informels, ou en voie de structuration', *Le travailleur social*, Ottawa, 43 (1975), pp. 55–61.] In other words, if you make participants do sociogrammes at the end of group sessions, and you relate them to categories of intervention according to Bales's grid, one finds that those who are most select on the affective level as well as those who are most select on the functional level tend to function in one type of category rather than another; here there is a 'Gestalt' or 'pattern'. I have come up with interesting results, but ones I do not want to comment on here. What I am trying to see with you is whether it might be possible, in this type of group, by using procedures like those I have described—the psychoanalytic attitude of the monitor being preserved—whether, then, it would be possible to pursue a double objective: that of formation and the analysis of group phantasies on the one hand and, on the other, behavioural ranking and return to individual conduct.

DA: Why not!

GT: The question I would put to you is therefore the following: if as the sessions proceeded (twelve to fifteen sessions by the end of the week, each of an hour and a half, interrupted by a fifteen-minute coffee break) one gave the members of a formation group the results of this apportionment of their interventions according to Bales's twelve categories, would this return to the specific behaviour of each group member in addition to the monitor's interventions be liable to help the participants? Is this a tool (and I am not talking only of Bales, but of other possible observation grids, like that of Flanders, for example) that might not only allow group members to change in depth, but also help them to become more aware of what they are doing, since these documents provide a snapshot of the interventions they have made during an hour and a half? At the next session they could say to themselves, after having seen their results, 'I would like to do something different. I will try instead to make other kinds of interventions.' In other words, with this tool or others of its type, could an individual adjust and develop his behaviour in the most desirable possible way, relative to what the group wants and relative to his own objectives?

DA: I am delighted every time different scientific approaches obtain convergent results. Facts in general, and *a fortiori* human and interhuman facts, are of such complexity that they need to be scanned by several methods so that one has more chances to grasp all their richness and all the connections.

GT: But is it possible in a group to combine psychoanalytic work (for the monitor) and the use of these devices, this setup, juxtaposed to the analytic work?

DA: I cannot say, since I have not tried it. You offer me a choice between two models. . . .

GT: No, both at the same time. . . .

DA: If you offer me a choice between the two models, I would prefer to choose one rather than to mix both, and to take the risk that one does not know very well where that is going to lead. Participants are going to find themselves faced with two systems of information: one system of cognitive information, linked to theories of learning by experience and bearing upon behaviour, and a system of unconscious processes. In my experience, it is enough to present oneself as a

psychoanalyst and to state that the group will have a psychoanalytic orientation to obtain very different material.

GT: The very fact of saying that one is functioning as a
psychoanalyst is already an enormous intervention. This
conditions the material.

DA: The unconscious only reveals itself when it is solicited.
I do not mean that soliciting it is enough to make it appear,
for resistances can introduce their own tricks, but it will not
reveal itself unless an appeal is addressed to it. The supposi-
tion that I would make—for this is not a hypothesis in the
scientific sense—is that one part of the participants would
function at the cognitive level and another part at the level of
unconscious dynamics. What is more, they could change
level according to the evolution of the group.

GT: My own experience has shown that one register
always takes precedence over the other. This depends above
all upon the attitude of the monitor.

DA: Certainly.

GT: Nonetheless, the cognitive material exists, and for
subsequent research it is good to have at hand the results of
sociogrammes that we can relate to Bales's categorization.

DA: I adopted an approach of this kind during a long-term
psychodramatic intervention that I undertook for two years
in a caretaking institution. I was assisted by a non-partici-
pant woman observer, whose job was to take systematic
notes along certain guidelines. She then made an abstract of
the findings and reassembled them on sheets relating to each
participant at each phase of the evolution of the psychodrama group and at each change in the atmosphere and
functioning of the institution. We were able to make cross-
checks, some positive and others negative, between the

changes that I myself perceived as an analyst conducting the intervention, and what the sheet showed us about relative stability in people's conversation, and about the permanence in the meaning of their remarks and their demands. It became strikingly apparent that the psychodrama group evolved a great deal; the institution, a little; and each participant taken separately, not at all. Therefore the members of a collectivity would not have to evolve for the collectivity to change. Each preserves his or her personal relationship to the group object. By contrast, the climate and functioning of the institution are modified by the construction of a group psychic apparatus that encompasses in a more or less durable way these individual group objects. [This example is taken from my chapter on psychodrama in large groups in the collective work directed by A. Kaës, *Le travail psychanalytique dans les groupes* [Psychoanalytic Work in Groups], vol. 2 (Dunod, 1982).] The difference resides in knowing whether you are collecting material that is going to be abstracted afterwards and ultimately put back at the disposal of the participants, if only out of honesty towards them, or whether you are injecting the information in a continuous 'feedback' as you go along.

GT: Say that it is at people's disposal if they want to use it. . . . This raises another type of problem: when you are running a group, you sometimes obviously include psychodramatic technique.

DA: Naturally.

GT: The problem that arises, especially when one has opted for an analytic orientation, is to decide at which moment it is appropriate to pass into psychodrama in the course of a group session. You are departing from your role as an analyst when you take up however slight a directive attitude, since the chairs must obviously be arranged in a certain way, the play started or stopped, and so forth. The initiative comes from you who up until that moment had been observing analytic neutrality. Have you never encountered difficulties in the course of a group from introducing psychodramatic play?

DA: Moreno employed forcing techniques that I do not like. I do not force people to be spontaneous. I invite them to be. If they do not succeed, it is because they are hindered by resistances. The first task of psychoanalytic work is to analyse resistances. How are these relieved? By talking about them. Sometimes an entire psychodrama session is taken up with a discussion of the preliminary problems and underlying anxieties that are preventing the participants from expressing themselves spontaneously as the order of the day invites them to. Spontaneity will then be sought out, but it will not be artificially provoked; it will come out of psychic work internal to each individual, from inter-subjective work between the members of the group, and from the interpretative work that is proper to the psychoanalyst who is monitor of this group.

GT: Can you now give an example taken from your own experience of the way in which a group reaches autonomy and the constitution of its own psychic apparatus?

DA: This was produced during the psychodramatic intervention in a hospital unit to which I was alluding a moment ago. The majority of the nurses and teachers who had psychotic children in their care felt excluded by the institution's hierarchy, and they were trying to develop an egalitarian and fraternal sub-group with claims to self-determination. The example in question shows how a group psychic apparatus shared by the caretaking staff as a whole was constructed. This took place during the third of the six intensive series of sessions that I led. The theme for psychodrama that was proposed and played out was that of a hairdressing salon. It so happened that the group who played it was composed of a single man (a nurse) and six young women (instructors, teachers, or child care auxiliaries). The man, naturally, took the role of the proprietor. He tyrannized the girls who worked in his shop. I entered the salon as a client, asking for someone to cut my hair. The proprietor replied that there was no room, and that I should come back another time: thus the intervention of a psychoanalyst who was a stranger to the hospital was symbolically refused, a precondition for those involved taking responsibility for themselves. A primary teacher took the role of a trade representative who tried to sell her merchandise to the proprietor. All the other women in the sub-group took a role. Some were hairdressers, others were apprentice hairdressers, and still others were clients. Each interpreted their role in a very personal way. The collective commentaries that followed this play related sometimes to individuals, sometimes to the psychodrama group, and sometimes to the institution. In the first place, they revealed a fear faced with the evolution of the group, which was tending towards personal psychodramas of a less and less professional and increasingly psychoanalytic character. In fact, as the participants explained, a hairdressing salon is a place where one talks about one's life. Others pointed out that people were afraid that psychodrama would give them new heads, and that they would not recognize themselves any longer when they left. Others replied that it was also beautifying themselves in order to live better. In the second place, this hairdressing salon related to the institution. An atmosphere of disorder reigned, reflecting decisions made by the doctor in charge, which were experienced as arbitrary, and their consequences. It is also a place where hairs are split [Fr. *couper les cheveux en quatre*]: an allusion to the complex psychological work that the staff were invited to do with the children at the hospital. The hierarchical structure of the institution was also symbolically represented: the proprietor of the hairdressing salon was the doctor in charge; the hairdressers were the nurses and teachers; the apprentices were the child care auxiliaries; the clients were the children cared for by the unit; and as for the trade representative, this was an allusion to the psychoanalyst who came to 'sell' his method of psychodrama to the institution. Finally, there were moments of individual insight on the part of participants, which some came out with at the time and others kept to themselves or confided to me by taking me aside. *In short, this hairdressing salon symbolized the formation of a group psychic apparatus.* Once constituted, this group psychic apparatus was able to subsist outside psychodrama sessions and meant that in meetings of the unit, exchanges between staff members and the medical hierarchy became more active and effective once again: case discussions, measures that needed to be taken, and the organization of tasks began to go better. But this group psychic apparatus was not constructed once and for all. Subsequent series of sessions enabled it to be maintained and strengthened.

A life in its setting

G T: I do not know whether you want to talk about this, but we do not know very much about the circumstances of your life at the moment. You are married, and you have two children, I believe. What does your wife do? Is she an analyst like you? Does she have a profession? Or is she simply the mother of your children?

DA: Indeed, I am married; I met my wife during the last year of my secondary education at the Collège Jacques-Amyot at Melun.

GT: How old were you then?

DA: She was sixteen, and I was seventeen. We took the baccalauréat in philosophy together, and we then met up again a year later at the Sorbonne. We both hesitated to undertake medical studies, which would have fit better with our sense of vocation, but which represented a long and expensive detour to reach what interested us. And then we had to earn our living fairly quickly. We studied philosophy first of all, then psychology. We were married in 1947, during our studies. My wife then trained as a speech therapist. She specialized in language re-education with children. For a while she was also involved in the re-education of aphasic adults. She published notably a long article on the problems of stammering in a collective volume that I directed, *Psychanalyse et langage* [Psychoanalysis and Language] (Dunod, 1977). Her article was entitled, 'De la Chair au verbe: mutisme et bégaiement' ['From Flesh to the Word: Mutism and Stammering']. She contributed some articles on femininity to the *Nouvelle Revue de Psychanalyse*. After I was well on in mine, she in her turn did a psychoanalytic training. She practised psychoanalytic psychotherapy with children at the Centre médico-pédagogique Édouard Claparède, and then at the Centre Claude Bernard in Paris. She is currently a consultant in speech therapy and in charge of the department of psychotherapy at the Hôpital de la Salpêtrière, in Professor Duché's child and adult psychiatry unit. Like myself, she has a psychoanalytic practice with adults, and both she and I see our patients at home, each in our own consulting room.

GT: When you lead a group, do you ever do so with her as co-monitor?

DA: Rarely. We have many points in common; but we have also made a point of preserving our differences. My wife has kept up activities as a child psychoanalyst and speech therapist. As for myself, I did collective psychodrama with children at the beginning of my career. Then I had a long experience of practice in the area of adult groups, for training in group psychology and interventions of psychoanalytic type in caretaking institutions. The only group activity that my wife and I have in common is a seminar on psychoanalytic technique for analysts training with the Association

Psychanalytique de France, to which we belong. Co-leading such a group as a couple creates a particular climate that seems to us to promote greater sensitivity to the unconscious in participants. We discovered this effect in the course of intensive psychoanalytic seminars that we co-directed for a week at the invitation of Argentinian colleagues in Buenos Aires in 1980.

GT: On the level of individual psychoanalysis now, would you say, since you must talk about it together, that your wife belongs to the same school of thought as yourself?

DA: We belong to the same grouping of psychoanalysts. The Association Psychanalytique de France does not impose a unique doctrine upon us because it was founded precisely in order to leave its members the greatest possible freedom of theoretical thought. We followed a training with masters that we ourselves chose, and which several times turned out to be the same. We write, though I more than she, but on more than one occasion she has provided me with a guiding intuition that I have given shape to, argued out, and developed. We read one another's texts (but not always); we discuss them together, criticize them, and perfect them. We are not always on the same wavelength to start with, but we generally get there in the end. My wife took an interest in Melanie Klein before I did, because of her experience of child psychoanalysis and her way of psychoanalytic thinking. It was through the group angle and on my wife's suggestion that I was in my turn inspired by certain of Melanie Klein's views.

GT: You have two children. . . .

DA: My children are no longer children. They are grown up and independent, and I have the pleasure of being a grand-father. They are both over 30. Both are married. They have chosen routes that are very significant in relation to their parents' professional orientation. After a detour through literary studies and the economic sciences, my daughter took her Maîtrise and D.E.A. in psychology, and then she went through medical studies and specialized in psychiatry.

GT: And your son?

DA: By contrast, my son found he had a gift for the so-called exact sciences (mathematics and physics)—perhaps in reaction to the psychologizing milieu in which he was brought up. He headed quite naturally for different studies from those that we had done. He worked his way up through the preparatory classes for the great scientific schools. He went to the École Centrale. He is an engineer and works for the civil and economic applications of nuclear energy in a research laboratory, on problems relating to the safety of the material at the core of the supergenerators that produce electricity. He is especially concerned with the mathematical modelling of the numerous parameters involved.

GT: What is interesting in these career developments is that your son adopted a route radically different from that of his father and mother, whereas your daughter engaged instead in a direction very close to that of her parents. . . .

DA: The children chose their destinies. I am glad that they did not take the same direction. They also needed to differentiate themselves from one another. But personal destinies are in part predetermined. My son was not named Pascal by accident. I have already explained that my first work of research was on the philosophy of Blaise Pascal and the edition of his *Pensées*. My wife and I called our son Pascal deliberately. For us, this name represents the ideal of a conjunction between science and philosophy. It is a wish that our son has doubtless taken up on his own account, while ridding himself of the psychoanalysm of his parents and our friends. As for our daughter, we had already named her

Christine by explicit reference to Queen Christina of Sweden, who invited Descartes and the great thinkers of her time to her court and to whom Pascal dedicated his arithmetical machine. The parents' ideals are conveyed in the children's names. I believe something is missing for children who have not received their parents' ideals, if only so that they can change them.

GT: When your children were young, you were already doing many things—you had a practice, you were teaching, you were writing. Were you able to make time, with your wife, to set aside for them?

DA: We had the feeling we were giving them plenty of time. They had the feeling that they were not given enough. . . .

GT: Popular imagery as you know represents psychoanalysts as people who take malicious pleasure in splitting hairs in four directions, especially when it would have been enough to split them in two. So what becomes of the children born to a couple of psychoanalysts?

DA: My wife and I aimed to differentiate our professional attitude from our family attitude. To be mother and father within the family, with our qualities and defects. To conduct ourselves first and foremost as parents, and not as psychoanalysts. Whether we succeeded is another matter. Nothing is more noxious, devaluing, and destructive than wild psychoanalysis within a couple or in a household. Having said that, psychoanalysts or not, parents have their character and reveal themselves as too permissive here, too frustrating there. They inevitably relive their own infantile conflicts with their children. Sooner or later, they are disappointing.

GT: To enlarge the discussion, what are we to say about those evening meetings at which analysts set about making speeches together, listen to themselves talk, interpret the slightest gesture or the smallest slip of the tongue, and hurl a shower of epithets at one another that literally freeze and paralyse the non-initiated?

DA: Like you, I detest such meetings. I mix moderately with analysts apart from a few colleagues with whom my wife and I are great friends.

GT: M Anzieu, another very delicate question. Is the rule of silence truly respected in analysis? Whether one likes it or not, a psychoanalyst is someone who must keep professional confidentiality, in the same way as a priest.

DA: Absolutely.

GT: Is this rule respected? Do you never say to one another at such meetings, 'Listen, I am going to tell you a good one! Here is what such-and-such a patient said, here is what he did . . .'

DA: The rule of professional confidentiality first of all concerns protection of the identity of persons in treatment. It is out of the question for us to say, 'I have so-and-so in analysis'. On the whole this rule is respected, and I maintain that it must be. We have a tendency when one of us breaches a confidence to react by saying something like, 'Keep that to yourself'. With tact and humour we bring him back into line. And if by accident one of us does learn the name of another analyst's patient, this is in turn kept as a professional secret. By contrast, it is not a breach of professional confidentiality when an analyst at a scientific meeting with colleagues reports and comments on a session with one of his patients (while giving no details that would make it possible to identify him), given the interest of this session for the progress of the treatment or because of the problems it has posed him. This is a precondition for a measure of scientific progress in psychoanalytic matters and is necessary for the training of young analysts. But this must always be done in such a way that the patient's anonymity is respected, and that what one says about him is in no way pejorative, ironic, critical, or devaluing. It should be explanatory and aim to improve the psychoanalyst's work and facilitate the patient's development.

GT: What measures are there, not preventative this time but corrective, that can be taken against fellow workers of yours if, once they have been admitted to a psychoanalytic society, they become known for their lack of seriousness about this rule of silence? Are there ways of stopping them on this slope?

DA: Breaches of the rule of silence, and even more of the rule of abstinence, like every repeated breach of professional conduct, can result in friendly warnings or even sanctions, for example withdrawal from the list of members of the association.

GT: That seldom happens, M Anzieu. . . .

DA: It is exceptional. What is more, such measures are not blazoned about publicly: discretion is imperative there, too.

GT: Is the material setting of importance for your work?

DA: I am very sensitive to certain settings. It is not without reason that I have emphasized, following Winnicott and others, the importance of the environment for a child's development, as well as for that of a group. For my psychoanalytic work in Paris I have a rather small room, rather too filled with books, rather dark, but giving out onto a rather calm cul-de-sac, an intimate room that promotes mental concentration and the necessary secret circulation between unconscious minds; the tiny road where I live is at once in the heart of the Latin quarter (I have lived in this quarter since the age of 18 and would not change it for the world) and on the periphery of the commercial and festive liveliness of the rue Mouffetard. The locals lead a provincial life there, a few steps away from the monumental Panthéon and sheltered from the litter of the Boul'Mich close by. On the other hand, although I conceive my books in Paris, I write them in my holiday house. My wife and I got into the habit, once our two children were born, of spending the summer in the south-west of France, on the Atlantic coast. We ended up by having a villa built on the top of a dune that overlooks the sea, on the edge of a pine forest; it is equipped to live in all year round. The sun drenches it with light until it sets. Vegetation surrounds us with its life, oxygen, colours, and smells.

GT: I would like to quote what you wrote in your note presenting yourself in preparation for this book. You wrote of yourself, 'In his public life, he liked three things: to produce reflection, laughter, and dreams. In his private life, he found satisfaction in one thing alone: being loved.' Being loved, yes—but what about loving?

DA: That sentence came to me spontaneously. I thought as I wrote it that I would be asked this question, this 'poser'. But I decided not to alter the phrase that my unconscious had dictated to me. It did not completely surprise me: I had had too much of the feeling, through the whole of my childhood and adolescence, of having been unloved by my mother.

GT: I would not like to insist upon it excessively, but your phrase is on several levels. I am trying to understand it. The reader will doubtless also try to understand it.

DA: I would not have talked to you about the richness, strength, and complexity of loving feelings as I did at the end of our sixth interview if I had not had personal experience of them, but I maintain that this question, when one broaches it